"Doug Alderson has spent most of his life exploring–and protecting–some of the most beautiful, remote, and mysterious places in Florida. *Wild Florida Waters* is organized as a paddler's guide with easy-to-follow instructions of where to go and what to see. But it is more than that. It is a celebration of a part of Florida most visitors—and many residents—never see, a celebration of what old-timers call the *real* Florida. To see it, to experience it as those who came before us, doesn't require much. All you need is curiosity, an adventurous spirit, the ability to paddle a boat—and this book."
--Warren Richey, journalist and author of *Without a Paddle: Racing Twelve Hundred Miles Around Florida by Sea Kayak*

"Through first-person accounts, Alderson has done a great job of informing the reader of the wonder, wildness and beauty of natural Florida. His stories evoke visions of relaxation and excitement, as well as serenity and a sense of adventure. The stories are punctuated with great humor and self-deprecation. A great read for anyone interested in spending time in Florida's great natural wilderness. It is past time somebody wrote a book of this caliber. A treasure trove of information for nature enthusiasts."
--Bill Richards, Executive Director, Paddle Florida

"As a native Floridian who has the opportunity to paddle in the state of Florida, I read Doug Alderson's new book *Wild Florida Waters* with great interest. His blend of history and personal anecdotes is both entertaining and enlightening. If you have an interest in the Florida outdoors and waterways I am sure you will enjoy this book as much as I did. Maybe this year I'll get the nerve to tackle the rapids of Big Shoals on the Suwannee River myself."
--Tom McLaulin, President, Florida Paddling Trails Association

Wild Florida Waters

Exploring the Sunshine State by Kayak and Canoe

Doug Alderson

www.dougalderson.net

ISBN-10: 1463669097
ISBN-13: 978-1463669096

Earthways Press
960 Towhee Road
Tallahassee, FL 32305

Cover photo: Cyndi Hunt pushes through wild rice on the lower Wacissa River.

All photos by Doug Alderson

*To all of my paddling companions, past and present,
and to those who seek to protect Florida's waters*

*Kelly Thayer, Mike Mendez and Georgia
Ackerman on the Wacissa Slave Canal.*

Table of Contents

Regional maps   1
Foreword and Acknowledgements   4
1. Ichetucknee Rattlesnake!   8
2. Swamped on the Suwannee   14
3. Banjo Music in the Ten Thousand Islands   30
4. Nightmare on the Sopchoppy   39
5. Shoal Challenges of the Withlacoochee North   47
6. Paddling through Hell   52
7. Alone in Hell's Half Acre   62
8. Hidden Passage   71
9. Pithlachascotee Hooter's   80
10. A Watery Thread through Time   84
11. Rawlings Country   95
12. Wild Rivers, Limpkins and the Mall   107
13. Rally for the Wacissa   116
14. Paddling Florida's Turtle River   120
15. The Almost Famous Graham Creek   126
16. The Lake of Canoes   135
17. Kissimmee's Gem   142
18. Canoe Fishing with Lucky Paul   147
19. Forgotten Coast Headwind   155
20. The Wild Wind of Apalachee Bay   166
21. Vicarious Paddling   182
22. Kissimmee River Dream   189
23. The Manatee Haven of Blue Spring State Park   195
24. Paddle Florida: Eco-tourism at its Best   201
25. More Than a Stream   210

26. Wekiva Wilderness   219
27. Florida's Mountain River   233
28. Pelican Island Pilgrimage   247
29. Clear Lake   253
30. What We Pass On   259
Bibliography   263

*Cypress angel on Devon Creek,
along the Apalachicola River.*

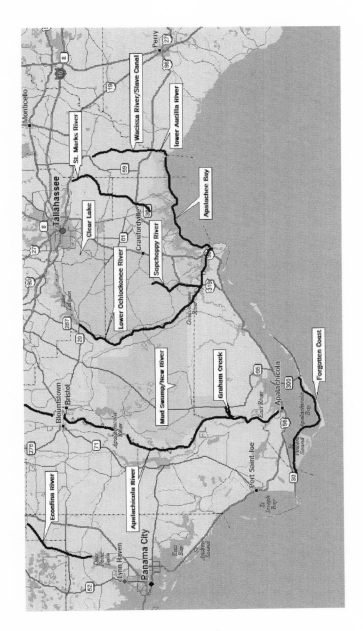

Featured North Florida waterways

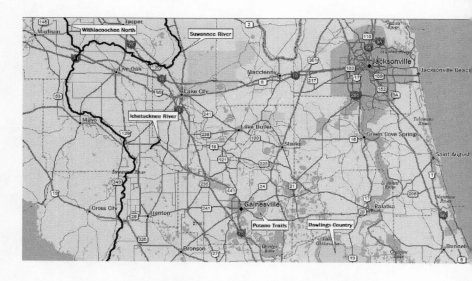

Featured North-central Florida waterways

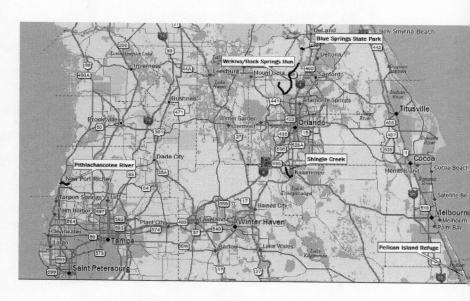

Featured Central Florida waterways

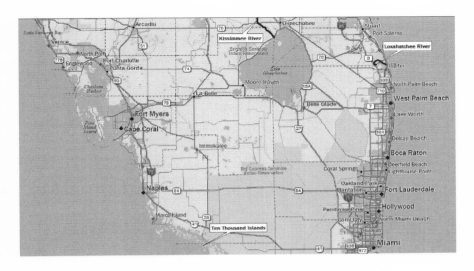

Featured South Florida waterways

Foreword and Acknowledgements

Let the names of Florida's rivers and coastal waters roll off your tongue: Ocklawaha, Chassahowitzka, Suwannee, Waccasassa, Aucilla, Wacissa, Sopchoppy, Withlachoochee, Loxahatchee, Homosassa, Pithlachascotee, Econfina, Kissimmee... If you've paddled these waters in a canoe or kayak, the Native American place names evoke winding streams and shaded hammocks, shimmering coastal waters and wild tree islands. Florida is made for paddling.

Numerous streams and rivers borne of springs and swamps are within easy reach of nearly every Florida city. Then there are the saltwater environs—thousands of miles of tidal creeks, bays, inlets and open water. The labyrinths of mangrove tunnels and marsh-lined tidal creeks invite discovery, along with historic vestiges such as Indian temple mounds, middens, lighthouses, and rubble from Confederate saltworks. A kayak or canoe is the easiest way to explore Florida's past, or to spot feeding birds and lounging manatees, or to cast a line for lunker fish.

Adventure often accompanies paddling, too, whether it's tipping over in the Suwannee River's Big Shoals rapids—twice—or surfing wind-generated waves while paddling the remote Apalachee Bay, or meeting up with a different form of "wild life" on a scenic waterway. Enough adventures fill this volume to delight armchair adventurers for hours. And where else but Florida can you paddle through a remote swamp and not see another soul, or meet up with a man who seeks to reenact an early Spanish raft voyage that ended in disaster?

Through all of the adrenalin, Florida's unsurpassed beauty and abundant wildlife are in the forefront, from the mangrove labyrinth of the Ten Thousand Islands to the springfed Ichetucknee River. Plus, useful how-to information at the end of each chapter will help readers plan their own paddling adventures.

Kayaking and canoeing is a growing outdoor pursuit in Florida, as evidenced by the establishment and success of several Florida "blueways" and other paddling trails over the past ten years. In Lee County alone, the number of outfitters has nearly tripled since 2003, thanks to the highly successful Calusa Blueway. Kayaking and canoeing is immensely popular in Florida, and a book such as this that covers the entire state appeals to both Florida residents and visitors. I certainly haven't covered all of Florida's wild waters—there are far too many—but I've included a good sampling of what's available. Links to detailed guides and maps to most of the waterways I've featured are provided at the end of the chapters.

I feel fortunate to have had the opportunity to explore Florida's waters since 1968 when I first moved from Illinois at age eleven. A Boy Scout canoe trip on the Suwannee, Santa Fe and Ichetucknee rivers (see chapter one) opened my eyes to the Real Florida, and I've been paddling ever since. For the past few years, I've been extremely fortunate to have been given the opportunity to map the 1,515-mile Florida Circumnavigational Saltwater

Paddling Trail for Florida's Office of Greenways and Trails, and to help coordinate Florida's many scenic river trails and blueways. Florida's waters seem a part of my blood and although many of these stories are humorous in nature, I hope to convey a strong message of conservation and stewardship.

If you are new to paddling, I urge you to first join a club or sign up for guided trips by outfitters. Take safety courses and buy reliable equipment. Obtain good maps and guides. Then, simply enjoy the wonders that are out there, and create your own adventures.

Acknowledgements

Florida's human population has certainly mushroomed in the last few decades, causing a strain on natural resources, open space and wildlife. Fortunately, some of Florida's most pristine waters have remained relatively intact. That is due to the concerted efforts of dedicated people who have carefully placed lands in public ownership, utilizing a series of state land buying programs over the years such as the Conservation and Recreation Lands Program (CARL), Save Our Rivers, Preservation 2000 and Florida Forever. Our state's natural environment would be in dire straits without these efforts, so thank you! May our land buying programs be fully supported, for our waters, fish and wildlife, and for all of us.

Earlier versions of some of these stories first appeared *Florida Wildlife, American Forests* and *Florida Sportsman*, and I would urge continued support for these fine publications. Additionally, a version of the chapter on the St. Marks River, "A Watery Thread through Time," first appeared in the *Between Two Rivers* anthology, and it also won first place in the 2008 Florida State Writing Competition in the previously published nonfiction article category. "The Wild Wind of Apalachee Bay" was a first place winner in the 2009 Seven Hills Writing contest in the creative nonfiction category and "Alone in Hell's Half Acre" was a second place winner in the 2010 Seven Hills Writing contest in the same category. "Forgotten Coast Headwind" won a first place excellence in craft award from the Florida Outdoor Writers Association in 2010. I thank these contests and associations for their support and for helping to keep me motivated.

Lastly, I'd like to thank the many folks I have paddled with over the past few decades, including family members, friends, work colleagues, outfitters and those active with the Florida Paddling Trails Association and Paddle Florida. Without you, this book would not have been possible.

1
Ichetucknee Rattlesnake!

"About noon of the second day's march from Charles'
ferry we reached an oasis in this desert, which broke upon
our vision like the fairy-land sometimes seen in dreams.
Itchetuckney was the name of this terrestrial paradise, for
such it seemed to our weary faculties."
--Jacob Rhett Motte, 1837, *Journey into Wilderness*

My first overnight paddling experience was in boy
scouts at age twelve—year 1969. My scoutmaster,
Ken, dreamed up an elaborate adventure whereupon the
troop would launch canoes at Branford on the Suwannee
River, paddle downriver to the Santa Fe River, then
paddle up the Santa Fe as far as we'd want to go for
several days. As it turned out, when we paddled up the

Santa Fe and reached the clear azure waters of the six-mile Ichetucknee River, the allure of cold spring water in summer was too much. We took a sharp left and paddled upstream against the swift current.

Ken asked me to be the keeper of the troop journal for the trip, perhaps sensing my future as a writer. I wrote exciting passages that detailed menu items for meals and the estimated mileage paddled each day, not exactly a treasure trove of information for future chroniclers of Boy Scout lore.

The Ichetucknee in those days was not protected in the environs of a state park like it is today. Tubers and canoeists alike enjoyed the river, and it was evident that both groups liberally guzzled beer while floating down the scenic stream. Empty beer cans were voluminous. Being boy scouts, we spent the next three days peering into the gin-clear waters, enthralled by the abundant fish and turtles and dancing ribbons of eel grass, and diving for beer cans. We filled our boats with them. When we found a tall mound on shore that had been collected by some other good Samaritans, we added our offerings to the pile in what could be looked upon by some future archeologists as a beer can midden of historic significance, should it remain intact.

Our real adventure was not in exploring the Ichetucknee's deep springs or shaded hammocks, however. It was in stumbling across a large diamondback rattlesnake near our camp that was as thick as my thigh and longer than any of us. It was a beast, the largest rattler I've seen before or since, and when it coiled, rattled and hissed, Ken deemed it a threat to our safety and determined that it should be killed. Now, this may not occur today, especially on public land and given the growing scarcity of large rattlesnakes in the southeast, but the 1960s was a different era. A venomous snake near a group of young campers was generally put to death for being none other than a venomous snake, whether showing aggressive tendencies or not. The rattler bravely held its coiled position while we ran about gathering large rocks in preparation for the stoning.

My herpetologist friend Bruce Means claims that diamondbacks are generally non-aggressive, and when left unmolested, they will soon go about their business and give people a wide berth. Bruce had been fanged before, but only while trying to catch large rattlers. On one occasion, he was proving to a companion how complacent rattlesnakes can be by purposely stepping on one with his right foot; it didn't coil or rattle. What he didn't realize at first was that his left foot was already bearing weight down on a different rattlesnake, and it never rattled or struck.

If we were Muscogee Creek or Seminole Indians, perhaps we would have reacted differently. The rattlesnake was *jetto mekko*, king of snakes, and custom forbade them to kill a rattlesnake. However, when naturalist William Bartram visited Creek and Seminole villages in the late 1700s, one group of Seminoles were more than happy to have him dispatch a huge rattlesnake in their village, and let him take on any negative karmic consequences that might result. "These people never kill the rattle snake or any other serpent," he wrote, "saying if they do so, the spirit of the killed snake will excite or influence his living kindred or relatives to revenge the injury or violence done to him when alive."

Our "battle" with the Ichetucknee pit viper lasted several minutes. We threw our stones with haphazard abandon while Ken made sure we kept a safe distance. The snake struck at each rock that came close. I admired its tenacity. If it would have simply ducked down and crawled swiftly away, that would have been the end of it, but it faced its multiple opponents with all of the force it could muster. After all, this was the master serpent of Florida. One would expect nothing less.

Posing with the rattler after the kill.
I'm the third one from the left.

When a couple of large rocks struck the snake in the head, it finally collapsed and Ken finished it off with thudding blows from a large stick. The battle against one snake had been won by a gang of boys and an adult. No human had been struck by the snake's fangs, but our adrenalin was pumping full force. Ken held up the lifeless body with both hands. The snake was slightly longer than he was, more than six feet. We had killed a worthy adversary, and it was beautiful. We took turns touching the rough scale-covered skin with the gleaming yellow, brown and black diamonds. Ken skinned the snake for a war trophy.

I'm not sure how many large diamondbacks live along the Ichetucknee today, but I know they are protected. And what about the beer cans? None are allowed in the park. In fact, no disposable items of any kind are allowed on the river in an effort to keep down litter and to keep bare feet safe from broken glass. The best time to paddle the river is any time other than summer, when people floating on inner tubes number in the thousands each day. In winter, the river is virtually abandoned and litter free, and completely undeveloped within park boundaries. I'd love to see a rattler again, just to know one is there.

If You Go

The Ichetucknee River paddling trail within the state park is about three miles. Many paddlers launch near the Highway 27 Bridge and paddle upriver and then back down. From Highway 27, it is about two miles downstream to the Santa Fe River. The waters are generally a clear 73 degrees year-round thanks to nine named springs and numerous unnamed ones. Collectively, the springs crank out an average of 233 million gallons of fresh water a day.

The nearest kayak and canoe rentals are only a quarter mile from the park's north entrance, Ichetucknee Family Canoe and Cabins, 866-224-2064. They also provide shuttle services and rent cabins and campsites. Call for details.

During quiet times on the river, kayakers can spot wading birds, wood ducks and river otters. The river's once eroded shores are now fully vegetated thanks to the park's strong conservation measures.

In 2007, park officials rescued a large diamond-back rattlesnake stuck in a fence that protected a rare snail habitat. It was proof that rattlesnakes are still present in the park and continue to play a vital role in the area ecosystem.

Paddlers meet tubers meet on the Ichetucknee River.

2
Swamped On the Suwannee

"Of all the rivers in America the Suwannee is the most romantic. It has a place beside the royal rivers of the world, though no New York, Paris, or London sprawls along its banks, and no torrential cataract appears in its course to challenge Niagra."
--Cecile Hulse Matschat, *Suwannee River: Strange Green Land*, 1938

Two alligator eyes peered from dark waters before submerging. The reflection of our canoe passed over the newly formed ripples and I envisioned the large reptile eying a wood paddle as it broke the mirror of blue sky and clouds.

My partner Randy and I had paddled lazily down the famed Suwannee River for three days, having begun our trip in Fargo, Georgia, just below the vast Okefenokee Swamp headwaters. We had marveled at old-growth cypress and live oaks, enjoyed the bright green of budding spring leaves, and spotted several slow-moving alligators. Now, porous limestone shelves and cliffs lined the shores, the river flow deeper and swifter as we dropped in elevation. Then, we passed a sign which read, "Danger—shoals one-fourth mile."

"I guess we'll see what hot-shot Florida rapids are really like," Randy said laughingly. He was from Atlanta and often paddled whitewater rivers in North Georgia and the Carolinas. This was his first Florida paddling trip. "We probably do bigger rapids when we practice rolling our kayaks on the Chattahoochee River."

"Big Shoals are the only Florida rapids that have claimed lives," I cautioned.

"Look," Randy said mockingly, pointing to large raptors along the horizon, "buzzards are already gathering overhead."

Another danger sign loomed ahead: "Shoals—500 feet."

"Listen to that roar," I said nervously. The sound of whitewater was unmistakable, even if it was in Florida. Normally, the Suwannee River has a quiet song, peaceful and gentle as it winds lazily 235 miles from the Okefenokee to the Gulf. It lives up to the lofty images portrayed by Stephen Foster in "Old Folks At Home." Foster chose to immortalize the Suwannee because it rhymed better than South Carolina's Pee Dee River, but he had never set eyes on the swamp-fed stream, and he had never imagined the churning Big Shoals rapids.

Randy's smile broadened as the roar of rapids grew louder. "Sounds just like Niagara Falls," he scoffed. "Panic, panic, class one-half rapids ahead!"

We rounded a bend and soon spotted the Suwannee's class III rapids, the largest shoals in this mountain-free state. Turbulence was frothing the dark, tannin-tinted water a foamy white. Black limestone boulders jutted out from three major drops in elevation and two huge logs lay trapped against them. It was an awesome display for one so used to quiet subtropical rivers—mirror-like slow-moving water giving way to raging whitewater and coarse rock.

Big Shoals at medium/low water levels.

Randy refused to portage gear around the rapids. "This is where we would take little kids to practice on the Chattahoochee," he said, although I noticed a distinct lack of playfulness in his voice.

I took a deep breath as Randy steered us into Big Shoals. White water was soon brawling around our gunnels. The canoe dropped suddenly and took in water, narrowly missing a boulder. "My God!" Randy cried. "I can't believe this."

More water sloshed into our boat as we shot over another drop. By now, we were like a rocking bathtub filled with water. We gave up on paddling and simply held onto the gunnels for stability. "I can't believe this, I can't believe this!" Randy kept shouting.

Going over the third and final drop, the current rolled us over like a water-soaked log. Gear washed out and swirled in the foam. We tried to hold onto the slippery overturned canoe, shaking from adrenalin and cold water. We were on the wrong side of the canoe and it nearly pushed us under, so we swam around to shift our position.

Swirling in the middle of the river, two men and a blue canoe with gear strewn as far as one could see, we began to laugh, the danger having past. "I haven't had this much fun since I can remember," Randy exclaimed. Only then did he inform me that his nickname was "Roll 'em over Randy," conceived when he swamped a former boss while canoeing the upper Chattahoochee River. As we spent the next hour retrieving our sopping gear, I wondered if Randy's seasoned whitewater friends back home would hear anything of this misadventure—whipped by a Florida river!

Round two at Big Shoals occurred a few years later, this time in a river kayak. Once again, spring rains had swelled the river and made the shoals an impressive sight. Two friends and neighbors, Dennis and Maria, were my guides. I was a novice whitewater kayaker; they were experts, and they gave me useful pointers and fitted me with a life vest and helmet.

As I paddled into the rapids, it didn't take long for the current to whip my kayak sideways and flip it. I quickly pushed out of the kayak and, feeling helpless, bounced over the limestone bottom. My hip slammed into a boulder. "Climb on top of the boat," Dennis yelled. I scrambled atop the overturned craft just in time to ride over the last big drop. The kayak hit several rocks; I was glad it wasn't my body.

Once again, Big Shoals had triumphed, but this time I wasn't laughing.

Drying out on the bank and emptying water from the kayak, I nursed my bruised body and ego while watching Dennis and Maria play in the shoals. Whitewater paddling was certainly not my forte, or was it just the Suwannee?

Kayaking below the shoals, I enjoyed a river of high banks framed by blooming pink and white wild azaleas. Mammoth trees seemed to grasp the steep banks with tightened fists lest they be washed away like I was at Big Shoals. It was an image of power intertwined with tranquility, an appropriate metaphor for the Suwannee River.

Most of my excursions along the Suwannee involve peaceful canoeing or hiking, or dropping by the annual Memorial Day weekend Florida Folk Festival at White Springs, or visiting with friends such as Steve Williams. Steve has been living in a riverside home near White Springs since 1978. The lifetime Floridian ran a canoe livery service for several years and now operates an art gallery. The 1,300-mile Florida Trail traverses his front yard, part of a sixty-mile section along the river. Steve is also founder of the Florida Panther Society, a non-profit organization dedicated to furthering the reintroduction of the Florida panther to suitable wild areas of the Southeast, areas that could include the Suwannee River valley.

I talked with Steve on the back porch of his home/gallery that overlooked the river. We sipped cold water from mason jars as we watched hummingbirds take turns at his feeder. The Suwannee and all that it represents is Steve's passion, perhaps best exemplified by an excerpt from his poem, "Rivers' Journey":

Come with me from the deep night
to sunrise, into sunset and touch all
those places remembered
down the river to the Gulf of Mexico.

Know her sweetness, bathe in
her healing waters and as the eagle,
bear and manatee, drink of
life from her springs and seeps.

Then you too, will be a part of her,
of the river, if you take the time
to love the Earth and care for her
as you take the Rivers' Journeys.

Steve enjoys sharing the Suwannee's wonders with
visitors, as long as they show a sense of respect. "I want
people to come here and feel a sense of place for this
place," he said. "I look on nature as being the base and
source of life. If you tread softly, it returns ten-fold."

Below White Springs, the Suwannee makes a huge
horseshoe-shaped curve of almost a hundred miles.
Several springs feed into it, including the mineral-laden
Suwannee Springs. Once a major health resort from the
Civil War to the 1920s, the springs area had a succession
of four hotels, a bathhouse and several cottages. A spur
line along the Savannah, Florida and Western Railway
brought thousands of visitors annually, lured by promises
of healing waters that could cure everything from kidney
troubles to nervous prostration. The resort faded with the
railroad, and the last hotel burned in 1925. Only ruins
remain of the complex, but the springs itself is now public

property. Visitors can swim inside the original stone walls of the bathhouse and discover for themselves if the spring water, which smells like a lost Easter egg, can cure what ails them.

I once visited Suwannee Springs on assignment for *Florida Wildlife* magazine. The agency overseeing the magazine was the Florida Fish and Wildlife Conservation Commission and I was in one of their cars, a white Ford Taurus sedan. Pulling up to the dirt parking lot, I was pleased that I had the place to myself. As I unloaded my camera gear, a rattletrap Buick approached with music blasting. It was filled with young people, and when they opened their doors, marijuana smoke wafted out. They were laughing and having a good time—so much for peace and quiet—but they suddenly stopped, glanced at my yellow state license plate, and then at me. As if by some unspoken agreement, they jumped back into their car and roared away, leaving me smiling through their dust. They obviously thought I was some form of law enforcement officer, a rare mistake. I was grateful.

Alone at the spring, I sought to test its healing properties. Prayerfully, I sprinkled the sulfurous spring water onto a sore shoulder; bursitis had inflamed the joint. On my drive home, I reached into the back seat to retrieve my daypack and, to my surprise, no pain! In fact, the shoulder didn't bother me for several weeks after that. There's something about those healing springs...

A smattering of other springs bubble forth in this upper half of the river, and there are also rapids at certain water levels other than the infamous Big Shoals. In 1881, author Kirk Munroe began a 1,600-mile journey in a 14-foot sailing canoe at Ellaville, just below the confluence of the Withlacoochee River. Almost immediately, he encountered trouble. "Left Ellaville at 7 o'clock, rainy and thick fog," he began in his journal. "Canoe very deeply laden. A mile below town ran three rapids—foundered in second, had to jump overboard to save canoe from upset. Shipped considerable water and got blankets wet. Went into camp five miles down Suwannee River on left bank. Sun came out and I hung everything out to dry. Stayed quietly in camp all day. Very wild country and have not seen a human being either on river or shore."

Munroe finished the Suwannee portion of his journey without further incident, replenishing supplies by purchasing milk and sweet potatoes from river residents and hunting squirrels.

Evening on the lower Suwannee at Old Town

Near Branford, the Suwannee becomes broader and large springs are more numerous. They make an already picturesque river seem like a many-jeweled necklace.

About 260 freshwater springs dot the Suwannee River basin, pumping more than 2.8 billion gallons of water a day. Dubbed the Springs Heartland, it is one of the largest concentrations of freshwater springs in the world. They are ideal cooling off spots when paddling in warm weather.

Naturalist Archie Carr, before his death in 1987, long visited the Suwannee's many springs. "When I think back through the little gems of natural landscape that have stirred me, none had the dreamlike quality the springs had before they were found by the masses of people who admire and remodel them today," he wrote in *A Naturalist in Florida*. "The springs I remember most vividly were the ones you traveled to down long, sand-track roads through dry pine hills. The first sign of something different was the dark green of a clump of broadleaf trees; then you saw the spring boil like a blue gem in its setting of green hammock, its water tumbling up out of its deep birthplace and roiling the surface with little prisms that sprayed color from the slanting light of the morning sun. Where the surface lay quiet, the deep places were some shade of blue, the current-washed bottom was snow white, and the rest of the basin was spread with polychrome gardens of half a dozen kinds of submerged water plants. The clarity of the water was absolute. You could watch a crayfish juggling a dead minnow forty feet down, or a stovewood catfish chewing water as he peered from his lair in the mouth of a side boil."

In recent years, nitrate pollution in the springs and the resultant algae and exotic plant blooms have been a pesky problem, but another ominous threat is water quantity. The historic White Sulphur Springs at White Springs, once a sacred place to Native Indians and one in which a healing spa was built around in the 1800s, has had little or no flow since around 1980 due to a drop in groundwater levels and pressure. "The spring is gone for all intents and purposes," said David Still, executive director of the Suwannee River Water Management District. "It is now a green slimy cesspool." The reason? The groundwater divide between the upper Suwannee and water hungry Jacksonville has been steadily dropping and shifting to the west since the 1930s. That means that a drop of rain that reaches groundwater in the upper Suwannee basin will most likely flow east towards Jacksonville and not towards the Suwannee River. Human population growth and a steady increase in demand have intercepted the upper Suwannee's lifeblood.

"We found out that we are not as water rich as we once thought," said Still. "Over twenty percent of our water is now gone. We have nothing but true hard core data [since 1936], but people don't want to believe it. If we don't get it under control, it will limit our growth, our agriculture and our water supply. We have to use water more efficiently."

Fortunately, springs along the middle river have been less affected thus far and the spring-runs make side trips off the river interesting and refreshing. When the river level is normal or low, the springs are usually a cobalt-tinted blue, revealing huge cavernous cracks in porous limestone bedrock. At flood stage, however, the river inundates the springs with dark tannin water. Then, the pressure created by floodwaters causes many springs to reverse their flow, causing them to draw water into the aquifer.

Floodwaters follow the path of least resistance, indiscriminately inundating buildings in the Suwannee's floodplain. The river deposits huge logs and debris in treetops that make post-flood visitors wonder if some giant has heaved them there. In reality, the giant is the Suwannee, a sleeping giant. During a dry period, one can walk across the upper river from shore to shore. At flood stage, however, the river can be life threatening and cause massive property damage. Paddling the river at flood stage is not recommended. And to avoid having to pull boats across shallow stretches of the upper river during dry periods, make sure the river gauge at White Springs is above 52 feet. The gauge can be found on the Suwannee River Management District website.

Amos Philman has seen the Suwannee swell and recede countless times during a half-century of living along the river. I met him at the 270-acre Hart Springs Park and Campground, owned and operated by Gilchrist County since the late 1930s. Being the park manager, Philman enthusiastically showed me recent improvements at the park, including primitive camping areas and aggressive steps to halt erosion. The park includes a fully-enclosed pavilion that is often booked on weekends from late spring until fall. "Family reunions are our bread and butter," Philman said. "Of course, I'm kin to most of the folks around here, so it's a lot of fun for me."

Just below Fanning Springs along Highway 19, the Suwannee passes the largest remaining unaltered tract of hardwood forest in the Suwannee River basin. It is part of the 3,877-acre Andrews Wildlife Management Area. Two national registry trees, the Florida basswood and winged elm, are found here along with four Florida champion trees—persimmon, Florida maple, bluff oak and river birch. Early loggers mainly focused on the area's virgin cypress and floated them to sawmills via the river highway, leaving other old-growth species untouched in the Andrews tract.

From the virgin hardwood forest, the Suwannee makes its way past the final large spring along the river—Manatee Springs. This region was home to the Seminole village of Talahasochte, one that William Bartram visited in 1773. Bartram provided a detailed glimpse of early Seminole life, and he was especially impressed with their canoes. "These Indians have large handsome canoes, which they form out of the trunks of Cypress trees (*Cupressus disticha*), some of them commodious enough to accommodate twenty or thirty warriors," he wrote. "In those large canoes they descend the river on trading and hunting expeditions to the sea coast, neighboring islands and keys, quite to the point of Florida, and sometimes cross the Gulf, extending their navigations to the Bahama islands and even to Cuba: a crew of the adventurers had just arrived, having returned from Cuba but a few days before our arrival, with a cargo of spirituous liquors, Coffee, Sugar, and Tobacco." In return, the Seminoles traded deerskins, furs, dried fish, bees-wax, honey, bear's oil and other items.

The downfall of the Seminoles along the Suwannee began in 1818 when Andrew Jackson and a huge force of regulars, Tennessee volunteers, Georgia militia and Creek allies attacked villages of Indians and escaped slaves downstream at Old Town. The Seminoles dispersed but eventually returned, prompting the building of Fort Fanning near Fanning Springs during the Second Seminole War in 1838. The fort guarded a key crossing of the river and was a base for operations to clear out Seminoles in the region. Most Indians were eventually deported to Oklahoma while a small band ultimately survived in a swamp even deeper than Okefenokee—the Everglades.

Even before the Seminole era ended, steamboats and paddlewheelers began chugging up and down the river. The boats would usually go from Cedar Key, ten miles south of the river mouth, to as many upriver towns as water levels would allow. Some of the boats served as mobile general stores for river residents, selling or trading goods and merchandise. In the latter half of the 1800s, the boats carried cedar logs from the Suwannee region to Cedar Key's sawmills. One boat, the *Madison*, was scuttled by Confederates at Troy Springs during the Civil War to keep it from falling into Yankee hands. Its skeleton can still be seen resting on the bottom of the 70-foot deep pool.

But through it all, the canoe—now made of metal, fiberglass, carbon fiber and sometimes cedar strips—has remained a steadfast form of transportation and leisure. And in the late 1900s, another modified version of an ancient craft found its way to the Suwannee—the kayak. I know two people who have paddled the entire Suwannee, one in a canoe and the other in a sea kayak. The canoeist took 62 days. "I wanted to get to know the indigenous people," he said, "the ones who live along the river. When I met someone interesting, I stopped and stayed a spell."

The kayaker often paddled 40 to 45 miles a day because he was alone and "didn't have much else to do." He simply enjoyed the different scenes that each new bend offered.

The two experiences highlight contrasting goals of a long distance paddling trip: to experience a river or coastline mainly from the cockpit of a kayak or the seat of a canoe, or using the slowness of the craft as a means to explore something broader, such as local culture. Most paddlers enjoy a bit of both, and the Suwannee is a river that can deliver.

After Manatee Springs, the Suwannee makes its final run to the Gulf of Mexico, passing through the Lower Suwannee National Wildlife Refuge. The wide river mouth boasts expansive watery vistas, marsh-lined tidal creeks and small tree-covered islands. This is where the Suwannee releases freshwater and nutrients—its lifeblood—to a hungry Gulf. In return, the river takes in mullet, sturgeon, manatee and a host of other aquatic life forms. The Suwannee provides cold weather sanctuary for these creatures along with spawning and feeding areas. It is an age-old exchange unaffected by man-made dams and structures.

In order to protect the Suwannee's unique qualities, the Suwannee River Water Management District has been purchasing land and development rights from willing landowners. They have protected more than 125 miles of river frontage and 48,000 acres of Suwannee floodplain. It is an impressive feat when considering the conservation history of the 1970s, when local opposition defeated several federal attempts to protect the Suwannee through the national wild and scenic rivers program. The land purchases are helping to protect the river, and make any river journey more enjoyable.

I'd like to paddle the Suwannee's entire length at some point—slowly and leisurely—and make that third try at Big Shoals.

If You Go

The 265-mile Suwannee River offers a wide variety of scenery, springs, history and excitement. Whether paddling a couple of hours or the entire river, the trip will be memorable.

The Suwannee River Wilderness Trail, a linear state park that runs from White Springs to the Gulf, is unlike any other in Florida. Through a network of public and private facilities and outfitters, rustic cabins have been erected at convenient intervals, enabling paddlers to stay overnight in relative comfort. There are also screened pavilions with ceiling fans that are ideal for summer camping. Paddlers can also primitive camp on sandbars and other public land along the river, but they should first notify the Suwannee River Water Management District for a free special use permit: 800-226-1066 or 386-362-1001.

In all, the Suwannee Wilderness Trail includes six river camps, eight state parks and a host of public and private facilities, including small river towns that serve as trail hubs. Since 2005, when trail development began, annual visitation at the state parks along the river increased by 50 percent and the annual economic impacts of the parks have nearly doubled. This has boosted local economies while still allowing the region to maintain its authentic Old Florida character, part of an increasing awareness among eco-tourism advocates of promoting sustainable destinations.

Paddlers utilize the Suwannee Wilderness Trail year-round, and groups such as Paddle Florida feature bi-annual trips for up to 200 paddlers where participants are fed, educated and treated to nightly musical entertainment. Paddle Florida has also branched out to offer trips in other parts of the state (see Chapter 24).

To learn more about the Suwannee Wilderness Trail, along with local outfitters, log onto http://www.floridastateparks.org/wilderness/. Paddle Florida information can be obtained at http://www.paddleflorida.org/.

Launch along the Suwannee River at White Springs.

Bow view of the Ten Thousand Islands.

3
Banjo Music in the Ten Thousand Islands

"Down in the mazes of the Ten Thousand Islands, one will sometimes meet men who turn their faces away and will merely smile if you ask them their names. Sometimes they kill men whom they fear are after them, and occasionally they slay each other either in a drunken quarrel or for the purpose of robbery."
--Nevin O. Winter, *Florida the Land of Enchantment*, 1918

As part of my job mapping a sea kayak trail around Florida—the Florida Circumnavigational Saltwater

Paddling Trail—I had to scout the Ten Thousand Islands in Everglades National Park. This was one area I didn't want to venture into alone. I wasn't worried about people since the area's infamous desperadoes were largely a thing of the past. I worried about becoming lost. When you're sitting in a kayak, with a three-foot high visibility, the maze of tidal creeks and mangrove islands can all start looking the same.

My choice for a partner was Dean Rogers. Dean is a GIS mapping expert with the state's Office of Greenways and Trails. He's a skilled navigator and fun to be with, even in a pinch. While in the Keys the year before, we had a run-in with the law right after dinner in a Marathon restaurant. We were walking along Highway 1 to a discount store when a police cruiser abruptly screeched to a halt in front of us, lights flashing. "Hands on the hood!" screamed the young officer.

"What's going on?" I asked, approaching him. Dean and I were certainly not threatening looking, in my estimation. We were clean-cut, of medium build, with pleasant voices. I was tanned with a swarthy moustache, and Dean had a ruddy Scotch-Irish face underneath his all-American baseball cap.

"Hands on the hood!" the officer screamed again, opening his door as a barrier between us. It was then that I realized he was dead serious. He likely had a gun trained on us from behind the door.

So, with little choice, Dean and I complied. While we were waiting for the officer's next move, I whispered to Dean, "I don't know about you, but I'm clean."

Dean's eyes widened. "So am I," he stammered.

"But they might see I had a speeding ticket twenty-five years ago," I jested.

Soon, another police cruiser arrived with blue lights flashing. This was getting spooky. Perhaps they had a tip about terrorists bent on blowing up the two blimps on Cudjoe Key that beamed a free world television station to Cuba. In that case, we could be held indefinitely without a trial.

We were asked to produce driver's licenses, and after a few more minutes of hood hugging, we were set free. "There are two guys matching your descriptions who have been leaping out in front of traffic," explained the officer. "Sorry for the inconvenience." With that, he sped away, along with the other officer. Leaping into traffic? Did we look like suicidal maniacs? Dean and I were left to catch our breath and ponder the absurdity of what had just happened. It was a quirky case of mistaken identity. Just then, we spotted two young guys across the street, running erratically through a parking lot—the likely suspects.

In the Ten Thousand Islands, at least there were no highways or parking lots. After receiving permits at the Everglades City ranger station, we embarked on a three-day kayaking adventure. We met several canoeing and kayaking groups as they paddled in different directions. Some were heading for the 99-mile wilderness waterway just past Chokoloskee, while others were aiming for various coastal islands, as were we. All of the groups, and the rangers we met, had one thing in common—none were from Florida. While friendly and outgoing, most of the people hailed from New Jersey, Minnesota, Illinois and various other northern states. This was a national park after all, part of Everglades National Park, which meant that most visitors and employees were from someplace else. In that sense, nearly all of South Florida was becoming like a national park.

Most of the campsites in the park are large and can accommodate more than one group, so we were not surprised to see other campers along the sand beach of Rabbit Key. We landed and immediately introduced ourselves to three women from Iowa. They fidgeted nervously, so we told them we worked for the state of Florida and were checking out the islands for a sea kayak trail around the state. That didn't seem to help. "We have some men with us who are out paddling," assured one of the women. "They're coming back later."

"And there's a good camping spot on the other side of the port-a-potty," chimed in another. "There's not much room left here."

Feeling miffed, Dean and I paddled over to a cleared area downwind from the odiferous port-a-potty. "Didn't those women seem a bit paranoid?" Dean commented.

"Yes," I agreed. "I think they heard banjo music."
"Banjo music?"

I explained to Dean how the term was derived from the movie *Deliverance*, in which four canoeists meet up with hog-loving locals, and one of each party end up getting killed. "We are the only ones out here who have southern accents," I said. "They got spooked." Dean nodded. He was born and raised in North Florida's Fort Walton Beach—more southern than most parts of Florida these days—and I had adopted an accent from being in the Sunshine State since 1968. It was another case of mistaken identity. Instead of drug-crazed youths jumping out in front of traffic, we were now ax murderers—in kayaks, all because of our accents, and the fact that we were males.

On several occasions, at boat landings and at campsites accessible by road, I had heard banjo music. The strings were plucked by rowdy locals who had had too much to drink and were gunning cars and trucks, flinging bottles, blasting country music and screaming rebel yells. At one forest service campground I visited, a guy whacked maniacally on a live tree with an axe because his girlfriend had broken up with him. The banjo music played loudly that time. To my knowledge, however, I had never played the banjo music myself.

Maybe the Iowa women had heard about the desperadoes who once lived in the Ten Thousand Islands and assumed we might be their offspring. The collection of outlaws included the Hermit of the Ten Thousand Islands who allegedly had an island hideaway with slaves and a harem of women. But the most infamous renegade was Ed Watson, immortalized by Peter Matthiessen in his trilogy of novels, *Killing Mr. Watson, Lost Man's River* and *Bone by Bone*. Watson had allegedly killed Belle Starr in Oklahoma and a man in Arcadia before calling the Ten Thousand Islands home in the early 1880s. He continued to have various run-ins with the law for attempted murder and alleged murder—trouble just seemed to show up wherever he went.

Evidently, Watson had a habit of hiring people and not paying them at his farm on a chunk of uplands called Chatham Bend Key that he had purchased from a widow of another outlaw. When the crops were all in, cords of buttonwood gathered, and the cane juice had been squeezed, boiled down into syrup and packed in tins, the workers demanded pay. At this point, Watson thought it best to offer early retirement by knife or gun rather than part with scarce cash. It was a business decision. A new crew—usually consisting of transient men with few family ties and some who were wanted by the law—could be easily hired the next season. Watson may have killed as many as fifty laborers, some buried and later uncovered on the property, but perhaps many more weighted down and sunk to the bottoms of waterways and swamps.

Finally, in the fall of 1910, the fine citizens of Chokoloskee had had enough. They were tolerant of moonshining, smuggling, hunting birds for their plumes and other illegal activities. And if a man wanted to hide out from the law in the remote maze of islands, creeks and swamps like the Seminoles, that was fine—no questions asked—as long as they didn't murder folks for no good reason. Enough was enough.

So, when Watson tied up his boat at the town's boat landing, a crowd gathered and Watson was accused of killing another of his hands. They demanded his gun. Watson's short temper flared. He raised his shotgun and pressed the trigger. Unknowingly, he had purchased water-damaged shells from Smallwood's Store in Chokoloskee a few days before, so the gun misfired. The crowd, using good shells, then opened fire. It was as clean a community execution as you'll find in Florida's history. One witness observed that he had never seen a man so dead. Watson's body was towed behind a boat and quickly buried on Rabbit Key, the same mangrove island of our campsite, but it was later moved to Ft. Myers to rest alongside his wife's grave. No need to lure trouble from the afterlife.

The fictional happenings in *Deliverance* seem tame when compared to Ed Watson.

Walking around Rabbit Key, Dean and I ran into the three women again. They were on a stroll in a tight cluster, like a quail covey. Dean and I kept our distance and were courteous. The women were friendly, but guarded—perhaps the ghost of Ed Watson had spooked them. Then, one of them said, out of context, "I know tae-kwon-do."

Yep, ax murderers, in kayaks. The soaring osprey was whistling along with *Dueling Banjos.*

Dean Rogers taking a GPS reading in Chokoloskee

If You Go

Florida's watery maze known as the Ten Thousand Islands falls under the auspices of two main government entities: The Rookery Bay National Estuarine Research Reserve and the Everglades National Park. If camping in the Rookery Bay section, which lies northwest of the national park, no reservations are necessary for the six designated primitive campsites. This section runs from Cape Romano to the national park border. Follow Leave no Trace guidelines. These campsites have no amenities other than solitude and fresh air.

Before you can camp in Everglades National Park, you must obtain a permit at the visitor's center in Everglades City (239-695-3311). Everglades City is located near the southern terminus of Highway 29. Everglades National Park takes no advance reservations by phone; you must arrive in person up to 24 hours in advance of your planned first night's campsite. There are numerous motels and cabin rentals in Everglades City, some of which are accessible by water. Advanced reservations are recommended. You can launch at the park visitor's center.

National park campsites range from chickees that have been built on pilings in rivers and bays, ground sites that have been cleared within the mangrove forests, and beach sites. Campfires are only allowed at the beach sites (below high-tide line). The mangrove ground sites tend to have more insects, but be prepared for insects anywhere in this region at any time of year. Best times to paddle are the winter months.

There is no fresh water at any of the campsites and drinking water should be tightly secured with food in kayak hatches at campsites. Raccoons in the Ten Thousand Islands are as attracted to fresh water as they are to food. The campsites are primitive, although some have chemical toilets.

Navigating through the Ten Thousand Islands requires a GPS unit and good maps and nautical charts. It is safest to follow marked channels. After reaching the coastal islands, navigation is easier since paddlers can skirt along the islands. Tides greatly influence water depth and currents, especially in the main channels. Try to leave Everglades City on an outgoing tide and return on an incoming tide.

For longer extended day trips through the region, check out segments 13 and 14 of the Florida Circumnavigational Saltwater Paddling Trail (www.FloridaGreenwaysandTrails.com). You can also plan loop trips of varying lengths through Everglades National Park by crossing back and forth between the 99-mile Wilderness Waterway and the coastal route. To do this, download the park's wilderness trip planner: (http://www.nps.gov/ever/upload/WildernessTripPlanner.pdf). Canoe and kayak rentals are available at Everglades Rentals and Eco Adventures in Everglades City, 239-695-3299. They also rent camping equipment and provide shuttles and resupply services by powerboat.

This is Florida's remotest region, so good planning is essential.

Kayaks on Rabbit Key.

4
Nightmare on the Sopchoppy

"Here where the water is red, silty and dark, like unstirred cranberry tea, the natives do not worship just any earthworm. The region is blessed by a worm with a Latin name, *Diplocardia mississippiensis.* It is not to be confused with the skinnier northern red worms whose ancestors came over with the settlers at Jamestown. The land now known as the Apalachicola National Forest was never settled because of its sandy soil; thus its native worm was never weakened by the European gene pool."
--Thomas Tobin, *St. Petersburg Times*, April 14, 2002

One chilly November morning, I helped an outfitter friend with a trip on the upper Sopchoppy River in Florida's Big Bend. Sopchoppy was corrupted from the original name *Lockchoppee,* signifying the red oak in the

Muscogee Creek language, and at least one Indian family lived along the remote river until 1904.

The upper part of the Sopchoppy River flows through the Apalachicola National Forest and is the most scenic, with tall sandy banks and huge cypress trees. But it can also be challenging if the water is too low, or too high. The river has numerous hairpin turns, log "strainers," and protruding cypress knees that can present challenges. On this morning, the gauge at the Forest Road 346 Bridge read twelve feet, meaning the river was on the high side and moving swiftly.

Our guests were three elderly people from Tallahassee and a father and daughter visiting from New York. Four of the guests rated themselves as beginners who had little or no kayaking experience, while the fifth guest was known for taking risks that often ended up with her submerging in dark and cold water. But it was the father and daughter that I worried most about. The father—wearing what looked to be brightly patterned pajama bottoms—had paddled a canoe once or twice and the college-aged daughter had no experience. "What about alligators?" she asked at our pre-trip gathering, her voice trembling.

"Don't worry, it's too cold for alligators or snakes," I responded confidently. Earlier that morning, the mercury had dipped to below thirty degrees Fahrenheit, and the high for the day was forecast to be in the upper fifties. Our biggest risk was for someone to fall in, one reason the outfitter and I stashed several changes of clothes in our kayak hatches.

"But don't alligators live along the river?" the daughter persisted, seeming unconvinced.

"Well, yes, there are alligators in virtually every Florida river," I said, "but we won't see any today." She still looked frightened. "I've seen hundreds of alligators while kayaking," I added, "and none have been aggressive."

When I spoke at a kayaking symposium in Washington State in 2008, alligator questions ranked number one, followed closely by inquiries about snakes and one about possible "aggressive manatees." Evidently, the handful of alligator attacks that occur every decade, usually as a result of people feeding the toothy reptiles, received press coverage that spanned the continent and lingered in the dark recesses of peoples' fears. Far more paddlers die every year from hypothermia after falling into frigid Pacific Northwest water, but we don't hear much about that in Florida. We would if killer whales suddenly decided to snack on paddlers, however.

The father chimed in, "I wanted to do something today that was better than going to the frigging mall. This is going to be fun." He playfully socked his daughter in the arm. She gave him a dirty look. The outfitter decided that father and daughter would share a two-person tandem kayak since the daughter also seemed petrified at the possibility of steering a kayak.

After going over a safety check, we drove to the river. In the van, the husky father made a stab at proving he was a tough guy who could handle a wild river. "I started taking this class in taekwondo," he began, "and I found I could beat these young guys because I knew how to fight. I grew up in the city and I learned how to fight on the street, and these young guys knew the moves, but they didn't know how to fight. I did pretty good until I went up against the black belts." Oh boy, Rocky takes on kayaking! The man ran a shipping business and I guessed by his demeanor that he could be a rough no-nonsense character. Was the daughter as tough?

After the outfitter and I carried the six kayaks down a steep slope to the river, we briefly studied the swift flowing water. "Phew, it's moving pretty fast," the outfitter told me. "Why don't you take up the rear and I'll take the lead with the father and daughter." The daughter's eyes grew wide when she saw the frothing dark water, while her father remained calm. The outfitter instructed everyone in the proper methods of steering a kayak. "Strap on your life jackets and keep them on," she said. "No exceptions."

Launching the group was no easy task since we tried to keep all of the guests' feet dry due to the cold weather. I was wearing waterproof socks and waded in knee-deep, and so did the outfitter. No sooner were we all safely on the water when we heard a huge splash. A pick-up truck had stopped on the bridge and dumped a deer carcass and internal organs into the river. At first I thought it was a human body. This was indeed a bad omen.

"Won't that attract alligators?" asked the father nervously.

I reasserted that it was too cold for gators.

Once floating downstream, the daughter immediately let out a shriek when the father steered them into a tree and overhanging branches. The outfitter pulled up alongside and guided them safely to the main channel, giving more instructions. When they hit another tree, the daughter did more than scream. "Dad, you're a fXOIing idiot!" He simply laughed and gently splashed her. She let out another string of profanities.

"See, isn't this better than the mall?" he asked.

"What the fX9k is wrong with you?!" she cried.

These playful "Leave It to Beaver" interactions occurred off and on until our lunch stop, when tempers calmed as we munched on finger food and brownies. After lunch, the adventure continued. "Hey Doug," said the father, "if you ever become single again, you'll be able to find out if you're compatible with a woman if you paddle one of these with her." The daughter rolled her eyes and said nothing.

One exciting distraction was a large buck swimming across the river and ascending a steep bank in two quick muscular leaps.

Fortunately, the lower half of our river section was almost free of obstacles, and by this time, the father was becoming more skilled at steering the kayak. The two shot out ahead. After ignoring requests to slow down, the outfitter instructed me to stay with them. The rest of the group was paddling proficiently and seemed to enjoy themselves, although they moved slowly.

As I caught up with the kayak racing duo, the daughter was still in a foul mood, even though they were now avoiding most of the overhanging branches. "When is this going to end?" she asked me.

"We're getting close," I responded. "Maybe another mile or two." The total distance for the trip was just over five miles.

She repeated the question at nearly every bend, especially when the sun dipped low and the temperature dropped into the forties. "Where is that bridge?" she asked in a beseeching tone.

"Soon," was all I could say. "Soon."

The father playfully tapped her on the head with his paddle. "F80k!" she cried. "God, you're such an idiot." I wondered what their family gatherings were like.

With each stroke, I prayed for the end to come, but no matter how much you wish for a bridge to appear, it will stay invisible until you've paddled the required distance, a type of mystical kayaking Avalon. "I'm ready for this to end!" the daughter shrieked. "I'm getting cold. I can barely feel my fingers."

"I'm sorry, I can't make it end any sooner," I said, exasperated. "Just a couple more bends."

A bridge was never a more welcome sight.

After the outfitter and I hoisted the kayaks up a steep embankment and loaded them onto a trailer, we drove the guests to their vehicles. In leaving, the father thrust ten bucks into my hand. "Thanks for all of your help," he said. I smiled and waved goodbye to these kind people and hoped they would return in warmer weather to experience some really big Florida alligators. Rocky versus a twelve-foot reptile, now that would be a sight!

If You Go

The Sopchoppy River can be paddled in sections. The upper river as described here, from Oak Park Cemetery Bridge to Mount Beasor Church Bridge (5 miles), should be attempted when water levels are above 9 feet according to the USGS Oak Park gage available for viewing online-- http://waterdata.usgs.gov/fl/nwis/uv/?site_no=02327100& PARAmeter_cd=00065,00060. Ideal paddling levels are between 9.5 and 11 feet. Numerous sandbars and log strainers will restrict passage when the water level is too low.

The Sopchoppy River is about 30 miles southeast of Tallahassee near the town of Sopchoppy. Take Forest Road 365 (River Rd.) north from Sopchoppy 5.6 miles to Forest Road 343. Turn left (west) to the Oak Park Cemetery Bridge. Access is on the northwest corner of the bridge with a steep climb down the bank to the river. Take out is at the Mount Beasor Church Bridge. Take Highway 375 west out of Sopchoppy about 3 miles and turn right onto Forest Road 343. Take the first right to the bridge after about a half mile. Access to the river, on the northeast side of the bridge, is also steep. An Apalachicola National Forest map would be helpful in finding these upper river access points.

If launching at the Mount Beasor Church Bridge, one can paddle five miles and take out at the Sopchoppy City Park or paddle another five miles and take out at the Highway 319 Bridge. The river tends to be wider and deeper in this stretch, allowing for more year round paddling. Paddlers can also float from the Sopchoppy City Park to Highway 319 (5 miles), although the river is wider with fewer sandbars. The nearest kayak rentals are about 20 miles to the east—The Wilderness Way, 850-877-7200, and TNT Hide-A-Way, 850-925-6412. For more on the Sopchoppy River Paddling Trail, log onto http://www.dep.state.fl.us/gwt/guide/designated_paddle/so pchoppy_guide.pdf.

The town of Sopchoppy is known as "the worm grunting capital of the world," so worms are a local bait of choice for fishing the river to catch "stumpknockers" and other panfish. For "worm grunting," a person pounds a wooden stake into the ground and runs a wide piece of iron on top of it to create a strong vibration. This brings the earthworms to the surface for easy gathering. To honor this tradition, Sopchoppy holds an annual worm grunting festival every April.

Sopchoppy River paddlers

5
Shoal Challenges of the Withlacoochee North

Many rivers at low water can be challenging and the Withlacoochee River North near Madison, with its numerous shoals, is no exception. On a warm July day, I joined my friends Georgia and Mike and four children for an eleven-mile paddle on the tannin-tinted river, the name of which means either "little great water" or "little river" in the Muscogee tongue.

Soon after leaving the public launch at the County Road 150 Bridge not far from the Georgia border, we noticed that the current was almost imperceptible—until we hit our first shoals. The flow really picked up then. Our kayaks scraped bottom. Then we hit the second one; a few more scrapes with a crunch thrown in. This was definitely a river for the plastic composite type boat—fiberglass not recommended.

Worrying about the shoals we were encountering, Georgia asked me to lead since there were young people in all of the other boats. "Expendable Doug!" shouted her then eleven-year-old son Cole, giving me a new nickname.

"More like expendable kayak," I shot back. Thus far, the rapids were too shallow to be life threatening. On the third shoals, I hit a cleverly concealed submerged rock head on. The rushing current turned my kayak sideways, tilting my open cockpit into the current and allowing water to rush in. I bailed out and tried to move the boat. With the weight of the water and force of the current pinning the craft against the rock, it wouldn't budge. The other boats stalled behind me, the children watching in concealed horror. "Avoid that rock!" I shouted, stating the obvious.

After several minutes of rocking back and forth, I finally managed to push the swamped boat downstream and empty it enough to get in. That's when I learned that the hatch cover on my kayak leaked, along with my deck bag, since water had been pushing against both of them with great force. My wallet was soaked, along with other items. I learned a valuable lesson—always put wallet in a sealed container, even if placed in a "sealed" deck bag. Not following my example, everyone else made it through with nary a scrape and we immediately landed for lunch on a nearby rocky beach where I was able to lay items out to dry. Like on the Suwannee's Big Shoals, it was proof again that my destiny lay not in pursuing whitewater kayaking.

Along the beach, the children and I had a wonderful time examining chunks of fossilized coral along the shore, rocks that would normally be submerged. They were a testament to Florida's oceanic past. The brighter red pieces were usually flakes from early Native American flint knappers, the by-product of crafting spear points and stone tools. No need for waste disposal permits then. Fossilized coral made for some of the premier flint knapping specimens in Florida. Often, they were a semi-translucent red or orange.

Georgia Ackerman and her daughter, Carly, on the Withlacoochee River North.

With lunch over, we embarked again and encountered shoal after shoal. Most of them required exiting the boats and pushing them through the shallow rocks. This extended our time quite a bit and we worried about not being able to avoid potentially severe late afternoon thundershowers. Still, we made time for water fights and moments where we were enthralled by high exposed limestone banks that were pocked with small caves and boulder fields strewn across the river bed. Roots of many large trees had knotted themselves into the steep embankments, clinging for stability and survival. "This river is completely different than it was last fall when I first paddled this," Georgia kept saying.

By the time we reached the clear cold spring at Madison Blue Spring State Park, our take-out point along Highway 6, we had exceeded our expected arrival time by three hours due to our slow progress. "This water level is only for experienced paddlers," Georgia concluded. "Towing boats is not fun."

So, the northern Withlacoochee—labeled an official "adventure river" in Visit Florida's paddling brochure due to the many shoals—is even trickier during low water. At the same time, the river's beauty will stir even the stoutest of hearts, and there is very little development, especially in the upper section. It is highly recommended for the adventure paddler.

If You Go

According to the Suwannee River Water Management District, the automated river gauge near our put-in (Pinetta) measured 53.53 feet on the day we paddled—a near record low. Flood stage measured at the same gauge was 79 feet, so we paddled at more than 25 feet below flood stage. Not recommended. You would need about one or two more feet of water to avoid portaging most of the rapids (55 feet or higher). To check

current conditions, log onto
http://www.srwmd.state.fl.us/water+data/surfacewater+lev
els/real-time+river+levels.asp.
For maps and descriptions of the paddling trail, log onto
http://www.floridagreenwaysandtrails.com.

A Florida Atlas and Gazetteer is recommended for finding the put-in. The shortest route uses some unpaved roads, so you may want to take the longer paved route, especially in rainy weather. From downtown Madison, head north 10 miles on Highway 145 to Pinetta, then drive almost six miles east on County Road 150 to the public launch southwest of the bridge.

The takeout for this upper section is at Madison Blue Spring State Park along Highway 6 ten miles directly east of Madison. The nearest outfitter for rentals and shuttles is about 25 miles east of Madison Blue Spring— the Suwannee River Canoe Outpost at the Spirit of the Suwannee Music Park just above Live Oak, 386-364-4991.

Young paddler on the Withlacoochee North.

6
Paddling through Hell

"Tate's Hell is a combination of twisting vines, stinking swamp water, eerie birds, unexpected quicksand, and grotesque trees a thousand years old. Its death-like silence is broken only be the shrill call of a crow, the frightened howl of an unseen animal, or the angry buzzing of a swarm of swamp mosquitoes. It is a wicked land where you suddenly lose your sense of direction and proportion—the sort of place that eventually would frighten you to the point of insanity."
--Bill Snyder, "They Call It Tate's Hell," *Florida Wildlife*, June 1950

Cebe Tate learned first-hand about the huge tangle of bogs, rivers and pine flatwoods just north of Carrabelle. While searching for missing livestock in the late 1800s, he became disoriented in the swamp. Legend has it that he lost his gun, was snake bitten, and wandered aimlessly for ten days. When he finally crawled out onto a Carrabelle street, delirious with fever and his hair now completely white, he croaked, "I'm Tate and I've been through hell!" The general area where he wandered was soon called "Tate's Hell"—wet, thick, almost impenetrable, home only to bear, panther and red wolf. North Florida's Everglades.

Today, visitors to the Tate's Hell State Forest must use a bit of imagination to grasp what Cebe Tate experienced. Before the state took over, private paper companies had ditched, drained and logged nearly the entire 215,000 acres. To get a true feel of Tate's Hell, one has to visit the Mud Swamp/New River Wilderness Area in the adjacent Apalachicola National Forest, part of Tate's Hell's northern boundary.

To describe Mud Swamp accurately, one needs a thesaurus to find synonyms for "impenetrable." It has no human-made trails. A hiker encounters walls of jungle-like vegetation that even a black bear would find challenging. There are also muddy bogs, twisting streams of dark water, and unparalleled primeval beauty.
To canoe or kayak Mud Swamp following the New River can be even more challenging. Countless logjams and then a disappearing river channel are par for the course. The way in is the way out.

Inducted into the National Wilderness Preservation System in 1984, the 8,090-acre Mud Swamp/New River Wilderness lies in the southwest corner of the Apalachi- cola Forest. The tannin-tinted New River flows into the area and is swallowed by a sprawling swamp of cypress, black gum, Atlantic white cedar, titi bushes, man-sized cypress knees, and mud. According to one Forest Service employee who tried to scout a canoe route by helicopter, the river becomes very "divergent" and ends up in a huge silt bottom mud flat with no clear channel. Trying to canoe through the swamp might result in a painful discovery—a canoe does not make for a good bed at night. Somehow, after several miles, the New River pulls itself together again to flow out of Mud Swamp and into the broader Tate's Hell. It's a stronghold of the Florida Black Bear, and it harbors other critters one might expect—alligator, deer, bobcat, river otter, wild boar... Rarely, if ever, does one find a Sunday picnicker.

This impenetrability is what challenged me most when I first started exploring Mud Swamp in the late 1970s. It's what lured me there, however infrequently, ever since. Something in our nature seeks to overcome obstacles. Things like mountains and swamps test the human spirit and inspire us to push beyond preconceived limits.

I once testified in Congress, representing several environmental groups, on behalf of Mud Swamp/New River and other areas. It was part of President Jimmy Carter's plan to identify and protect potential wilderness areas on public lands, dubbed RARE II. While controversy swirled around many wilderness proposals that year like water around cypress knees, Mud Swamp/New River stirred up little opposition. It was probably the best Apalachicola National Forest candidate at the time, and the Forest Service and Congress agreed. Under oath, I could attest to its wildness for I had poked along its edges on foot and by canoe and could never penetrate very far.

All of Florida was once like Mud Swamp—not necessarily wet and swampy, but wild. Now, with much of the state tamed, Mud Swamp survives intact because of its sheer impenetrability and because it happened to fall into the public domain. Perhaps it also survives because we need to know such places still exist, a living legacy of Original Florida.

Over the years, as I started raising a family and working a steady job in Tallahassee, my mind would sometimes drift to The Swamp. One winter day when the weather was cool and clear—ideal for exploring swamps—I spread out an Apalachicola Forest map and searched for new routes through the heart of Mud Swamp. There was a side stream that flowed into the swamp from the east, Cat Branch, and it appeared to connect up with the New River just below where the river re-formed. It was worth a try. If one could reach the New River at this point, it might be a clear float out of the swamp!

I garnered the help of an unsuspecting neighbor, Paul Force, and we brought his canoe (mine was too small for two people), and his truck (I didn't have one). It's easy to enlist another person's help for a crazy swamp exploring adventure, at least, for the initial journey. After word spreads, the mere mention of Mud Swamp or similar environs will elicit groans and snickers. I have rarely gone twice with the same partner. Even Lewis and Clark didn't team up again after their famous journey. History reveals a pattern.

Paul and I drove to Crawfordville, then bumped and jolted our way along thirty odd miles of unpaved Forest Road 13. This was Original Florida driving at its best—bone-jarring—just how it used to be in the age of backyard outhouses. Not everything about Original Florida is romantic.

When we neared the swamp, we headed south along another sand road until we reached Cat Branch. Indeed, the dark stream looked passable by canoe. With luck, we would connect with the New River and make a broad horseshoe-shaped journey through the swamp, ending at the now defunct Owens Bridge, maybe four miles from our embarking point. From there, it was a three mile walk back to the truck.

The tricky part about our plan was that I had no idea if the Forest Service map was accurate. In my many years of dealing with the Forest Service and outdoor enthusiasts, I never met anyone who had actually traversed the entire swamp. Perhaps Cebe Tate was the last one. Who knows where he wandered in those ten hellish days? I didn't much care, so long as we didn't repeat Tate's experience.

As Paul and I began canoeing down the narrow tannin waters of Cat Branch, we were surprised to see signs of "civilization." Trot lines dangled from overhanging branches. Obligatory beer cans lay trapped in swirling eddies. I spotted a discarded blue worm container. However, once we carried the canoe over the first fallen tree that blocked our path, signs of people quickly vanished. We soon found out why. More logjams awaited. Vines and spider webs entangled us as if we were prey. Dislodged arachnids soon covered our craft. Cat Branch would not be designated a state paddling trail any time soon.

"I hope we don't have to come back up this creek," Paul said, eliciting a moan. A tall wiry fellow who worked as a carpenter, his face was red from exertion. Though physical, this was not a paid job. It fell into the category of off-hours "fun."

"With luck, we'll find the New River," I responded optimistically, "and then we'll just float on through the swamp." We were rapidly approaching that "point of no return" during an expedition where almost anything that lay ahead had to be easier than turning back. I wondered if there was a scenic reward for all this effort, like the prominent view or scenic waterfall awaiting the mountain hiker. In Florida, it might be a hidden spring or a nearly forgotten Indian mound or gargantuan trees missed by loggers. Or maybe we'd encounter a bear, or panther.

After three or so miles of canoeing hell, the creek opened up into a large swampy pond with islands of moss-covered black gum trees. Several small streams entered the pond from the north. Could we be close to the New River? There was actually a dry bank where we could shake debris off our clothes and empty the canoe of sticks and spiders. We were pleased not to find the vast stretches of mud that had given the swamp its name. I assumed we were below that point.

Huge loblolly pines along the pond certified that loggers hadn't penetrated this far into the thicket, at least not in the past eight or nine decades. Also, many of the cedar and cypress trees we saw appeared to be original growth, although some were stunted, perhaps attesting to low nutrients or a pan of hard clay soil underneath. South of Mud Swamp, in the heart of Tate's Hell, grows an entire forest of naturally occurring bonsai cypress. Useless to loggers, the man-sized old-growth specimens, nicknamed "hat rack cypress," are fascinating to gaze upon and stand beside. A forest for gnomes. Even the former owner—a paper company—spared the unique place, perhaps realizing that pine trees would not fare any better than cypress in reaching harvestable sizes.

Paul broke out his fishing rod and made a few casts in the pond, with no luck. The weather was too cool, we felt. Still, it was as remote a freshwater fishing hole as you'll ever find in Florida and the possibilities of good fishing were there. Bass, bream, warmouth, stump-knockers, pickerel, catfish and, appropriately, mudfish, can all be caught in the Tate's Hell region. The best fishing is in spring, early summer and fall, while the prime time for exploring Mud Swamp is in winter, when pesky bugs and reptilian life forms are dormant and visibility is better. Still, as we were finding out, passage through the swamp is not easy any time of year.

When Paul and I paddled to the southern end of the pond, we found a narrow outlet that had a current. "The New River!" I cried. "This must be where it forms again." We paused in admiration, feeling kinship with those early explorers who had found the source of the Nile. My confidence level soared.

The New River, it turned out, was only slightly wider than Cat Branch. It also had its share of snags. At one spot, cypress knees were so thick that we had to hoist the canoe over them for more than forty feet. In three hours, I estimated we had gone four well-earned miles since our embarkment. I guessed that Owens Bridge was only about two miles away. At least, I surmised, we didn't have to go back the same way we had come.

After more challenging portages over and around cypress knees and logjams, the river suddenly fanned out in several directions through a thick, shadowy forest of cypress and gum trees. Each channel was only a foot or so wide and a couple of inches deep. It was a virtual maze. The canoe could go no farther.

On foot, we sloshed around to see if the larger channel re-formed. Trees were so thick that a compass was necessary, and we didn't dare go beyond shouting distance from each other. We were also worried about leaving the canoe and never finding it again. Since the sturdy craft wasn't mine, I didn't want a lost canoe to weigh on my conscience. Finally, we had to give up. Even if we did find the channel again, it was doubtful we could have squeezed the canoe through the thick forest.

"I bet the Indians never came here much," said Paul, discouraged and yet awed, "unless it was to get away from someone." Scores of people could have easily hid undetected, one reason the Seminoles evaded large armies so successfully. But I'd be willing to bet that Native Americans didn't take dugout canoes through Mud Swamp. They probably had different names for it, like "land of disappearing canoes."

Downing a bag of pecan/chocolate chip cookies like true modern explorers, Paul and I contented ourselves with simply staring at the incredible jungle of trees and tiny streams of water. Occasional peeks of sunlight turned the rivulets into silver ribbons. There was a sweet smell in the air--not from blooming flowers, but from the swamp itself. No plane, boat, car or human voice broke our reverie. Just birds and trickling water.

Maybe Mud Swamp swallowed the New River because rivers are always going somewhere, never stopping or slowing down, like some people. The swamp seemed to have swallowed us, too, or swallowed our restless urge to move forward. It resonated stillness, or, at best, slowness.

Paul and I were in no rush to leave, and the great swamp wasn't going anywhere.

If You Go

The best way to explore the Mud Swamp/New River Wilderness Area is by foot. Bring old shoes that you're not afraid to get muddy or wet. Chaps or snake boots are advisable to protect one's legs from sticker vines and unwelcome reptilian surprises. A compass, gps and machete are recommended and it's best not to venture in alone. One can poke in a ways by canoe or kayak from each end of the swamp on the New River before encountering numerous logjams. However, the New River below Mud Swamp is largely navigable in good water and makes for an enjoyable wilderness paddle. Several primitive campsites have been established by the Tate's Hell State Forest, 850-697-3734. A special use permit is required for the campsites.

Winter is the best time for a Mud Swamp exploration. Aerial photos can be helpful and an Apalachicola National Forest map is essential. Forest maps can be ordered by calling either the Apalachicola Ranger District at (850) 643-2282 or the Wakulla Ranger District at (850) 926-3561. Perhaps the easiest way to enter the area on foot is to park along Forest Road 120 at the southeastern end of the wilderness area at Owens Bridge. Or, you can reach it from the other end by taking Highway 65 to Sumatra and heading east eight miles on County Road 22. From Owens Bridge, you can follow a fishing trail in a northwest direction along the New River for a ways until both the trail and river disappear, whereupon you can follow animal trails in whatever direction you choose. No blazed hiking trails are allowed in the Mud Swamp/New River Wilderness Area in order to retain a true wilderness flavor.

Jim Lollis pushes through a nearly impenetrable titi strand in the Mud Swamp/New River Wilderness.

View from Goose Pasture on the lower Wacissa River.

7
Alone in Hell's Half Acre

"A man's never lost until he can't tell his right hand from his left."
--Ross Summers quoted in "They Call It Tate's Hell,"
Florida Wildlife, June 1950

Dragonflies arose en-masse as I drove up to the Goose Pasture launch on the lower Wacissa River. The multitude of mosquito hawks meant fewer biting bugs as I readied my kayak for launching. July can be a tricky time for paddling given the bugs and heat, so allies were welcome.

Across the marshy river, a solitary great blue heron on a branch spread its wings, seeming to beckon. This would be a solo excursion by kayak, a trip neither rushed nor overly planned. I would simply see what the day and river had to offer.

Once paddling downstream, I passed pickerel weed and duck potato, food plants for early native people. Small alligators submerged. Woodpeckers flitted past.

Beneath the water's surface, long blades of eel grass danced in the current. Mullet rifled underneath my boat. Everywhere—high, low and all around—movement drew my attention, while the lush river corridor seemed to enfold me in a peaceful embrace. Each paddle stroke brought forth a deeper sense of relaxation. My breaths came long and measured. Kayak yoga.

There is a point on many paddling journeys, even the short ones, when the waters are smooth, the paddling seems effortless and the setting is almost dreamlike. Exercise, beauty, fresh air and an open mind achieve this state—no need for medicinal spirits or Woodstock helpers. Turn off cell phones and BlackBerry's. Be in no rush, no hurry. Transcend troubles. Let nature be your tour guide.

Rounding a bend, I met a lone cane pole fisherman. His massive white beard gave him the appearance of a western gold camp survivor—Gabby Hayes in a johnboat.

"Are they bitin'?" I asked.

"Just little bitty ones," he replied. He didn't seem to care. What could be better than to drift down a wild river?

I've only met a handful of people on the lower Wacissa. Once I maneuver past fallen trees and a shallow rock strewn-stretch, it is primarily the domain of canoe and kayak. Maps label the swampy labyrinth of channels and floodplain forest "Hell's Half Acre." I'm not sure where the "half" came from. The area spans a thousand or more acres, most of it state-owned. And "Hell" is a relative term. If you're lost and it's storming and the bugs are hungry, then it's hell. If that's not the case, more pleasant adjectives come to mind.

Several places in the United States bear the name "Hell's Half Acre." Most are areas that are difficult to navigate, such as a 300-acre lava flow in Wyoming considered to be a geologic freak of nature due to its spires, pits, crevices and buttresses. One source claimed that "Hell's Half Acre" is meant to be the opposite of "the Lord's acre," a term farmer's once used as an area set aside for a cemetery or for growing crops to give to the church or to the poor. Several Texas frontier towns in the 1800s originally used the term for red light districts where prostitution, gambling, brawling and cockfighting were commonplace.

Open an atlas of North America and you'll find several other locations with the name "Hell" or "Devil" in the title. Some, such as Devil's Tower in Wyoming and Hell's Bay in the Everglades, are well known, while Devil's Dripping Pan and Hell's Hollow in Connecticut are more obscure. Connecticut might lead the nation in such names with thirty-four that stem from Puritan settlers in the 1600s, perhaps as a warning that the Prince of Darkness may be lurking in the then New World wildernesses. Florida has its share, too, such as the breathtaking sinkhole near Gainesville known as the Devil's Millhopper and the dramatic Devil's Den Sink near Williston.

Psychologist Will Taegel, in his book *Wild Heart*, sheds some light on these devilish naming practices: "The primordial mind gave names of beauty to such places. In our dominant culture we often repress the experience of profound beauty and mystery, so we demonize the natural place with a negative name. It is our strange way of trying to control ourselves and the environment."

What was Hell's Half Acre called before the arrival of Europeans?

Given its remoteness, it's no wonder that speculation centered on this region as the home of the famous "Wakulla Volcano." First seen by Native Americans and the Spanish, the tall column of smoke arising from the deep swamps in or near Hell's Half Acre was the rave of Tallahassee soon after the city was founded in 1824. It could be seen on most any clear day from hilltops, rooftops and the capitol rotunda, and also by sailors who used it as a navigational aid while sailing across Apalachee Bay in the Gulf of Mexico. At different times, it was rumored to be from a camp of Indians, runaway slaves, and Civil War deserters. Some reasoned that it was a constantly burning peat bog fire. But most people just called it "the Wakulla Volcano."

"It is the greatest physical phenomenon in Florida," Maurice Thompson wrote in 1882 in *A Tallahassee Girl*. "It is a standing temptation to inquisitive and adventuresome folk,--a constant taunt and banter which Nature flaunts in the faces of scientific explorers, and it offers the reward of fame for high achievement to whomsoever will solve its riddle."

Despite several high profile expeditions through the deep swamps, the source of the smoke was never found. Following the 1886 Charleston earthquake, one that shook the entire Southeast, the "volcano" disappeared, never to be seen again.

In contrast to the relative isolation of Hell's Half Acre, the upper Wacissa River near the head springs—ten miles upstream from Goose Pasture—can be a human zoo of motorboats, airboats and flotillas of canoes and kayaks on weekends. It is beautiful, yet almost too accessible. A paved road leads directly to a parking and swimming area. Goose Pasture and the lower river, on the other hand, involves a long trek on jarring stretches of unpaved roads. It weeds out the masses.

Aside from fire and brimstone, Hell's Half Acre is aromatherapy at its best. Willow, wax myrtle, red bay and spider lily all give off a sweet smell, especially on humid summer days. And with no powerboats able to navigate past the first downed tree, smoky boat engines are absent, and human-generated noises are minimal.

On many Florida rivers, especially in central Florida, you can never completely escape highway noises, even if enveloped by a leafy canopy. That's because highways often parallel river corridors. Not on the lower Wacissa. Highway 98 is several miles away. Only the distant rumble of an occasional pickup navigating a back road, or the drone of a passing airplane, disturbs the serenity.

For the most part, Hell's Half Acre offers the perfect opportunity to be completely alone. With minimal machine noise and lack of human conversation, natural sounds are more acute. Cicadas and katydids whir in treetops. Kingfishers scold in trilling tones. Suwannee cooters drop off logs. Leaping mullet slap the water and long garfish thrash the surface. Then there are the glimpses of creatures that remain stone silent—statue-like deer in the floodplain forest, juvenile black-crowned night herons perched on limbs, brown water snakes draped over branches. If one is paddling or drifting quietly, many of nature's creatures simply choose to remain still.

When paddling alone, I feel a stronger kinship with early dugout travelers. It's as if the river easily spans the centuries as it spreads into the swamps—a liquid time machine. By necessity, those early people had to view the river as their grocery store, but I suspect they also came here for the same reasons I do—for spiritual sustenance.

Even though I rarely see other people in Hell's Half Acre, I am mindful that the land and waters were once home to untold numbers of people over millennia. Some of the oldest Paleo Indian artifacts in Florida were found along the Wacissa and in a nearby Aucilla River sinkhole known as Booger Hole, part of the larger Half-Mile Rise. The archeological site itself was labeled Page/Ladson. For several years, archeologists would dive the sink and make tiered excavations in the muck, sifting through silt to find pottery, stone tools, and bones of extinct animals that had been killed and butchered by Ice Age hunters. The entire Half Mile Rise once contained at least eleven complete mastodon and Columbian mammoth skeletons, although only three ended up in museums. The rest were taken by private collectors.

Here's how archeologist S. David Webb described the sensation of finding a mammoth radius bone that had been worked by humans in the dark water of Booger Hole. "As I turned it to view the convex anterior face, aided by the magnifying effect of the water, I was surprised to see that the outer cortex was worn almost through, partly exposing the marrow cavity," he wrote in the *Between Two Rivers* anthology. "And then as I examined the bone from left to right, pondering its origin, I realized that it was broken, and lacked the distal third of its length.

"At that moment a curtain of silt obscured my view. As I stared intently, waiting for the water to clear, a vision of a woman emerged from the darkness. She picked up an intact mammoth radius bone and began scraping a hide. She yelled strange sounds to a child seated nearby. Then she gave a hard thrust to the radius and I saw it snap. The longer piece fell to the ground; she stared at the distal end remaining in her hand. Even as I squinted in the back-scattered light to take in more of this scene, the woman and child faded into the darkness of the river sediments, and I was left astonished, cradling that same bone in my hands."

The mysterious images are not surprising; the region is one of Florida's cradles of civilization. Native people have lived, hunted and fished along the Wacissa and Aucilla for 12,000 to 14,000 years or more. When more established tribes formed, the Aucilla River became a dividing line between the Timucuan people to the east, and the Apalachee to the west. These tribes were eventually wiped out by European introduced disease and war, and Creek Indians moved into the area from Alabama and Georgia. They soon became known as Seminoles.

For many years, the Seminoles lived in relative peace with cotton and tobacco planters who had established themselves in the upper river valleys. But as pressure mounted to obtain more Indian land and to move the Seminoles to Oklahoma, depredations occurred on both sides. Swamps such as Hell's Half Acre became a base from which Seminole warriors could launch raids and safely retreat. As the Second Seminole War of the 1830s and early 1840s dragged on, however, most of the

Indians were eventually killed, relocated or driven south into the Everglades, Florida's largest swamp.

Ending a lone journey through Hell's Half Acre is an intuitive decision; there's no one else with whom to discuss the matter. On that July day, an alligator made the decision for me. I was exploring a narrow side channel when a massive beast the size of my ten-foot kayak burst forth from the shore. The water erupted as the gator sought a safe haven in the depths below. Instinctively, I paddled backwards. The narrow channel wasn't wide enough for both of us. That's when I decided to head back to Goose Pasture. The alligator was the lord of his domain, not me. Even though I've read accounts of people who bravely (or foolishly) rowed, kayaked or sailed across vast oceans, I feel more chicken when alone. Fall out and lose your boat in the upper Wacissa and you might receive help in minutes. In Hell's Half Acre, it might take days. When kayaking remote areas, the old adage of safety in numbers holds true.

I usually leave "Hell" feeling richer than when I came. For days and even weeks afterwards, I can close my eyes and easily visualize the swampy watercourses and my solo paddle. It's not just specific images or creatures that come to mind, but the entirety of the place—pure, vibrant.

I hope it will always remain difficult to navigate and nearly unreachable, where the occasional visitor feels as though he has been transported back to a pre-industrial age. "Hell" is in the eyes of the beholder.

If You Go

The easiest way to reach Goose Pasture and Hell's Half Acre is to drive on Highway 98 and turn north on

Powell Hammock Road. If traveling east on 98, this is the third road on the left past the Aucilla River bridge (about two miles). Signs point to Goose Pasture. Travel north on Powell Hammock Road about four miles and turn left on a graded limerock road and follow signs to Goose Pasture.

Once exploring the many side streams of Hell's Half Acre just south of Goose Pasture, take along a compass and GPS unit to help you find your way back. Be sure to take a GPS reading of Goose Pasture before you embark. Aerial photos can aid in navigation. For more about the Wacissa River Paddling Trail, log onto http://www.dep.state.fl.us/gwt/guide/designated_paddle/Wacissa_guide.pdf. The nearest outfitter is The Wilderness Way, located 30 miles west of Goose Pasture at Wakulla Station, 850-877-7200.

8
Hidden Passage

"We say about the Slave Canal that we go in and come out, as if it had a door hinged at either end, curtained with vines—Virginia creeper and wild grape. A passage. Rite of passage."
--Janisse Ray, *Between Two Rivers* anthology, 2004

"I've been down the Slave Canal at least twenty times," exclaimed my paddling partner, Georgia, "and I've never been lost like this."

Such exclamations are commonplace when dealing with the difficult-to-find north Florida waterway 30 miles east of Tallahassee.

The Slave Canal, built in the 1850s by African-American slaves to connect the Wacissa and Lower Aucilla rivers, is famous for its wild beauty, and for its challenges. In low water, numerous limestone rocks and logs inhibit passage. In high water, several side channels along the lower Wacissa before the canal divert the flow and can invite unwary paddlers to take a wrong fork. The result is a tangle of downed trees and branches and even more choices for side channels. The rugged maze only gets worse. That was the situation during my trip with Georgia. We stood on a muddy shore while our other paddling companion, Micheal (spelled "ea"), scouted a side channel on foot. "It looks like it opens up," he announced upon his return. "We should try that one."

We entered the channel and met with the same result—more snags, some nearly impossible to navigate through, even while wading and pulling our boats. "This can't be the way," Georgia sighed, flicking spiders off her shirt and hat. "I don't remember it ever being like this. This would be a great place for someone studying arachnids."

"Ow!" I yelped. "One just bit me." I had just rested my arm on my kayak when I received the jolt on my elbow. The black creature crawled away. I only prayed it wasn't poisonous.

Even with the confusion, we paused to admire centuries-old cypresses and other large hardwoods such as swamp maple and bay. A tangle of climbing vines had given some trees the appearance of a green leafy cascade. Water was cool and clear, most of it having originated from the Wacissa's fifteen upriver springs. Mullet darted away like miniature torpedoes. We had seen several alligators. This was as wild as anything Florida has to offer, a true bush paddler's paradise. As an old saying suggests, it's not the destination, but the getting there that counts.

In late spring, the area's wildness causes some paddlers to avoid it. April and May is alligator mating season, and yellow flies can be pesky.

We backtracked to the main river channel near Goose Pasture and carefully tried again to determine the correct path to the Slave Canal. "The canal entrance is just past a big cypress and a wood duck box," Micheal said, "and the river widens at that point."

"And I heard that the FWC [Florida Fish and Wildlife Conservation Commission] recently put up a sign pointing the way," I added. Most of the river corridor was purchased by the state in 2000 and 2003 and added to the nearly 50,000-acre Aucilla Wildlife Management Area.

The Wacissa River, including the Slave Canal, was designated a Florida canoe trail by the Governor and Cabinet in 1970. It is now one of forty-three legislatively designated Florida paddling trails.

We raced downstream in the swift current. "This looks very familiar," Georgia said. "I think we're on the right track." We spotted red plastic flagging tied to overhanging branches, but we had seen similar flagging along some of the other channels, so that didn't help. Everything seemed to be going smoothly, however. Bright red cardinal flowers and purple-flowered pickerel weed lined parts of the comparatively wide waterway—more than fifty feet across in some places—and we spotted the occasional white blossoms of duck potato and swamp lily. Tiger swallowtail butterflies added movement and more color.

Just when it seemed that the rest of our trip would go smoothly, we reached a vegetative wall of wild rice, so thick that it appeared impenetrable. "This is weird," Georgia said. "We did this trip in April and this wasn't here. How could it grow up that quickly? We must be in the wrong place." We backtracked again, explored other side channels, and finally decided to retreat to Goose Pasture as our time allotment was running out. After all, we did have other things to do in our lives besides paddling. "I am humbled by the water's flow and nature's changes," Georgia concluded.

"At least the clouds have kept the weather cool," Micheal said optimistically. "If we had to spend the night out there, it wouldn't be that bad."

In past years, several paddlers have spent the night looking for the Slave Canal. Before the sign was posted, many have overshot the entrance and ended up in the

Aucilla River, paddling until they literally ran out of river. The river swirls underground in a huge sinkhole. It's commonplace for the Aucilla. From its origin near Boston, Georgia, the Aucilla plays a disappearing act several times before rising for the last time at Nutall Rise, just above Highway 98 and less than six miles from the Gulf, not far from the terminus of the Slave Canal.

Friends of my parents missed the Slave Canal entrance several years ago. By the time they realized their error and ended up in Half-Mile Rise, part of the disappearing Aucilla. The sun was dipping low, and it was too late to paddle upstream back to their launch spot at Goose Pasture. They quickly learned that a canoe makes for a poor bed.

The reward for finding the Slave Canal is wild beauty.

I have successfully paddled the Slave Canal on other trips, and did so with a GPS unit only five days after my failed attempt. To her credit, Georgia also successfully navigated the maze to the Slave Canal the next month. A navigable channel did exist through the wild rice expanse. You had to push through the first line of rustling rice sheaves to see it, and then the channel was obvious the rest of the way. The Wacissa doesn't reveal its passages easily, especially in summertime, and conditions change from season to season and year to year.

Once on the canal, the lush swampy wilderness and occasional sightings of wading birds, bright-colored warblers, alligators, wild turkey and deer make for an enjoyable trip. You almost forget that this lush waterway was built by human hands with shovels and pick axes until you spot stacks of moss-covered limestone rocks and boulders lining the canal. It is an eerie reminder in this more "enlightened" age. Slaves were forced to labor in wet humid conditions, fighting bugs and malaria, and contending with all sorts of misery and discomfort. Nature has almost erased signs of that toil. Almost.

The canal was an attempt to open a shipping channel for cotton, tobacco and other goods, built during a period of canal fever spawned by completion of the Erie Canal in 1825. But alas, the Slave Canal's full potential was never realized. It wasn't deep enough, and railroads were soon established in the region. Today, mostly nature-loving paddlers enjoy the fruits of that early labor, along with Gulf-spawned striped mullet. Mullet schools are everywhere.

At one point, the FWC, as part of a statewide effort towards racial sensitivity in regards to geographic names, proposed renaming the waterway "Cotton Run Canal."

The Jefferson County Commission and several individuals familiar with the canal, including African-American leaders, opposed the name change. In January of 2006, the U.S. Board on Geographic Names agreed with the opponents, citing a lack of local support for the change. The Slave Canal remains the official name, serving to remind visitors of the men who built this sometimes paradisiacal waterway.

Appropriately perhaps, the Slave Canal is not an easy waterway to navigate. The entire trip from Goose Pasture on the lower Wacissa to Nutall Rise on the Aucilla near Highway 98 is only five miles, but it can take four to five hours, sometimes longer. If the water level is low, you'll scrape limestone rocks and shoals in several places. Snags are numerous at any water level and it takes skill and coordination to pull boats over huge logs without slipping and getting wet. The most challenging part can be near the bottom where tidal influence is evident. At low tide, rocks are covered with dark mud, and a long shoals area is too shallow to paddle. Paddlers must carefully pull their boats through the uninviting slippery goo. Snags are easy compared to that mess.

I've also been on the canal when it's overcast and raining. Without the sun, the swamp forest and water appear darker and more foreboding. I don't want to leave the security of my kayak, but then I have to stop and pull over a snag, stepping into unknown depths. It's more difficult to suppress primal fears of creepy crawly things—sharp-toothed alligators, snakes, spiders. Did I mention the many spiders? And then there are the echoes of those poor souls who dug the canal. I imagine them lingering there in the dislodged boulders. Perhaps a part of them, their sacrifice, has never left the canal.

Amidst the shadows, however, I often spot white-tailed deer. It's difficult to be gloomy around spry deer. That also goes for the leaping mullet making their way up the narrow channel from the Gulf of Mexico like southern salmon. No one knows for sure why they jump. Perhaps it's for the sheer joy of living! Smells come out more in the rain, too, especially sweet aromas of willow, red bay and brilliant white swamp lilies.

After a Slave Canal rainstorm has passed, sunlight envelops the swamp and highlights a dazzling array of color. Leaves, flowers, mosses—all seem to leap out in glistening brilliance. It is then that I realize why I came, and why I will return again and again… assuming I can find the entrance!

If You Go

The easiest way to reach Goose Pasture—the closest access point to the Slave Canal entrance—is to drive on Highway 98 and turn north on Powell Hammock Road. If traveling east on 98, this is the third road on the left past the Aucilla River bridge (about two miles). Signs point to Goose Pasture. Travel north on Powell Hammock Road about four miles and turn left on a graded limerock road and follow signs to Goose Pasture.

The take-out point at the Nutall Rise Landing is easier to find. Take the first road to the north on the east side of the Highway 98 bridge over the Aucilla River and drive less than half a mile to the landing.

For more information about the Slave Canal and Wacissa River paddling trail and to view a map, log onto http://www.dep.state.fl.us/gwt/guide/designated_paddle/Wacissa_guide.pdf.

The GPS point (in decimal degrees) for the Slave Canal entrance is N30.1829/W83.9686. A sign may or may not be present. The nearest outfitter is The Wilderness Way, located about 19 miles west of Nutall Rise at Wakulla Station, 850-877-7200. They also lead guided trips down the canal.

Hand-dug boulders piled along the Slave Canal.

9
Pithlachascotee Hooter's

The Pithlachascotee River in central Florida, 'Cotee for short, is the only designated Florida paddling trail that terminates at a Hooter's restaurant. So, when I joined my friend Ed and two retired companions, whom I shall call Bob and Ray, on a six-mile paddle down the winding stream, I started hearing about it soon after we embarked from the Grey Preserve.

We found the 'Cotee River to be wild and scenic in the upper section, lined with palms and live oaks. After only a mile, however, we were floating along the manicured shorelines of downtown New Port Richey. Several riverside parks came into view and it was fun to watch children running and playing along grassy strips atop seawalls. We also passed a couple of hundred parked boats and we were glad this was during the week and not on a busy weekend. Urban rivers are the least fun when dodging boat traffic, especially when large wakes bounce off concrete seawalls.

Just past Highway 19, the huge orange Hooter's letters came into view and I stupidly informed my companions that I had never been inside a Hooter's. The two senior men were incredulous. "You've never been to a Hooter's?" Bob said. "Now we have to go." Suddenly, I was about to be educated in the ways of women for the first time.

For most of my life, I considered the idea of eating or drinking while ogling scantily clad waitresses as a bit sexist and exploitive, and I would have never had any luck convincing my liberated past girlfriends or my current wife to join me. After all, didn't this sort of debauchery lead to the moral decay and downfall of the Roman Empire? Were we next? But there were other considerations. I was a heterosexual male and my maleness was being challenged by two older members of the species, and my wife wasn't around. And so after we landed at the concrete boat ramp and loaded up our kayaks, the orange gates of Hades were cracked open so this choirboy could slide in.

Bob and Ray ordered a pitcher of beer as they compared the visual significance of different waitresses. They talked like college fraternity brothers. A dark haired beauty seemed to be their favorite. Sipping my obligatory beer, Bob and Ray began regaling Ed and me with tales of their prowess on bicycles. They would sometimes pedal a hundred miles in a day, having built up their stamina over time. In their 70s, they would have put me to shame on wheels. Thank goodness they weren't bragging about their stamina in bed, although I worried that this subject was forthcoming.

As our cute waitress brought them a second pitcher—they could out-drink me as well—Ray asked if the waitress could pose for a photo with me since this was my first visit to a Hooter's. She smiled and agreed. I felt like a fifty-year-old virgin in a cathouse.

When Ed and I bid farewell to our gray-haired companions, we decided to drive back to the Grey Preserve and do some more paddling. Ending a paddling trip at a Hooter's somehow didn't feel satisfying, so we paddled upstream as the falling sun kissed treetops with golden light. This was Old Florida only a few miles from urban congestion. Not a person could be seen; only vine-tangled branches and aromatic spider lilies. It was here where the full name of the river—Pithlachascotee— seemed to have more significance. The name means "river where canoes are made" in the Muscogee tongue, and it was easy to picture this part of the stream used by early paddlers. We stayed out until dark as the wildness helped me recapture lost innocence.

If You Go

The 'Cotee River is best enjoyed during the week since boat traffic can be heavy on weekends. Several put-in and take-out options exist in parks around New Port Richey. The river can be easily reached from U.S. 19. Nick's Park, adjacent to the Hooter's, is on the northwest side of the U.S. 19 Bridge. The nearest outfitters are Mad Paddlers in Tarpon Springs (727-944-4542) and Wind-N-WaterSports.com in New Port Richey (727-736-8663). For more information, log onto http://www.dep.state.fl.us/gwt/guide/designated_paddle/Pith_guide.pdf.

Paddling the 'Cotee with friends.

10
A Watery Thread through Time

"Sister, Mother,
And spirit of the river, spirit of the sea
Suffer me not to be separated
And let my cry come unto Thee
--T.S. Eliot

Some people yearn to hear symphonies in their head and compose great music. I yearn to hear a great river and listen to its stories.

I often paddle the upper St. Marks River east of Woodville, Florida, north of Natural Bridge State Park, late in the day. The river, divided into mirrors of shadow and light, lures me on. A heron or an anhinga, always a prominent bird, keeps moving ahead, reappearing at bend after bend before flying off as I approach. Fading sun rays illuminate centuries-old cypresses, weathered trees that have known the rap of ivory-billed woodpeckers and the fluttering wings of Carolina parakeets.

I often pause to watch water bugs etch their ever-changing designs on the river's surface. Every creature, eddy, and arching branch of the St. Marks is a masterful work of art, worthy of appreciation.

Once I paddle past moss-covered stumps of pilings from a long forgotten bridge and pull my canoe or kayak over the first downed tree that blocks most boat traffic, there are few signs of people. That's when I really listen. A part of me begins to touch something very old.

I sense mastodon, saber-toothed cat, Paleo hunter and dugout traveler, and wonder about their stories. How did native people regard this flowing lifeblood of water, the hues of which change from rich brown to red, yellow, and occasionally a clear blue, depending on rainfall? What did they call the river before seventeenth-century Spaniards christened it St. Marks after one of their religious saints?

I yearn for a longer bridge over the abyss of time. While barred owls give voice to the waning light, the presence of those vanished species and tribes seem as much a part of the river as the water itself.

Of course, the river speaks in a myriad other ways, appealing to many senses—murmuring eddies, the popping of bream and bass, choruses of frogs and cicadas and goodnight songs of unseen birds. Even trees and plants seem to speak: the canopies of Florida maple, cypress, gum, holly, water oak, ironwood, American beech and fragrant wax myrtle. The sweet smell of lush willow takes me back to my earliest childhood days of fishing along waterfronts. It is a pure aroma, fresh and cleansing.

The prevalent sweetgum along the shore often reminds me of a Creek Indian story. A group of women who were laden with many emotional burdens gathered daily beneath a large sweetgum and talked of their problems. Each day, as they talked, their burdens seemed lighter, until one day they felt the entire weight had been lifted. Intuitively, they realized that the sweetgum tree, their daily companion, had absorbed much of their pain. Today, in the woman's ribbon dance at the Creek ceremonials, some women carry a sweetgum branch if they are troubled and later burn it in a special fire.

Maybe it's the sweetgum, or the river, or all of it, but I feel lighter after I've paddled the St. Marks. If my burdens haven't been lifted, they don't seem as important. On occasion, I've spotted otters swimming the St. Marks, and cottonmouths and banded water snakes. Once, while driving along Highway 27 near the St. Marks River Bridge, just below where a series of streams converge to create the river, I braked for a Florida black bear crossing the highway. I began to wonder what wild foods a bear would eat along the river, where they slept, and where they would mate and den. I yearned to communicate with bears.

How does the St. Marks River differ from other Florida streams? I like to think of rivers as possessing natural, unaltered DNA. All rivers are unique; there are no clones. Each has its own stories.

Sometimes, if I feel ambitious and there's time, I'll paddle from Natural Bridge to Horn Springs, about three miles upriver. Horn Springs is often clear and blue and deep. I used to party there as a teenager, before the sand access roads were closed, but I look at the springs through different eyes now. Someday, if the land around the spring becomes public property, and it might, I'd like to help stem erosion along the worn banks, and fill in the moonscape of holes left by disrespectful people searching for prehistoric Native American artifacts. Law enforcement officers, spread thin, play a cat-and-mouse game with the illegal artifact hunters, who often wear camouflage clothing, use portable police scanners, and dig at night while wearing headlamps.

If I don't have time to paddle the river, I'll often drive to Natural Bridge and stroll along this forested land bridge, admiring the glassy reflections of a river slowed to a near standstill as it swirls underground. On one spring afternoon, I met an aged man, Detroit Holton, fishing the dark waters. Detroit's wrinkled face bore a look of concentration and hopeful anticipation as he eyed his red and white bobber. "When you're retired," he said, "you ain't got nothing to do so you come down here instead of going to your job. I catch bass, a bream or two, a speckled perch or two, cats, mudfish."

His friend, Jimmy Martin, chimed in, "I keep a fishing pole in my car because I can't stand to go around water and see someone else fishing."

I stood with the men for a spell, watching bobbers, before I wished them luck and quietly left. As I walked away, I heard most of a story Jimmy shared with Detroit: "This guy told me he was fishing here by himself and three guys popped up out of the sink. About scared him half to death. Then he saw they was wearing scuba gear and they came up from down river…" The two men erupted in laughter.

One year, I visited Natural Bridge on the first weekend in March. No fishermen lined the sink. Civil War reenactors had come from across the South to set up an 1860s-style encampment and to fire blanks at each other. Originally, it was here at Natural Bridge that General John Newton and more than five hundred black Union soldiers tried to cross Natural Bridge in hopes of occupying the Florida capital of Tallahassee. Nearly six hundred well-entrenched Confederates, mostly old men and young cadets, repeatedly drove them back. The Yankees, charging uphill, lost 148 of their number; the Confederates only three.

"Turtle Bob"Walker holds a loggerhead Musk turtle on the St. Marks River.

Below Natural Bridge, after the river rises for good at a place called "the basin," my friends David and Casey Gluckman built their wood home in 1980, setting it 350 feet back from the water. A winding boardwalk through an untouched floodplain forest gives their property a park-like atmosphere. If you're going to live on a river, they set a good example. I love to perch at the end of their boardwalk and gaze at the water.

David once told me about an age-old winter run of mullet he witnessed heading up the river. "I put my kayak in the water and mullet started exploding," he said. "The water was clear and I noticed that when I looked across the river, it was solid mullet from bank to bank, top to bottom. I paddled upriver and they were exploding in front of me just continuously, and it was solid mullet almost a mile upriver."

My own familiarity with the section of river below the Gluckman's house was firmly established by several annual moonlight canoe trips. They were our "junkets" for legislators in the 1970s and '80s when I lobbied for environmental causes with the Gluckmans. The river in this section was perfect for such a trip. It was wide, relatively free of snags, and completely wild until it reached the Highway 98 Bridge at Newport. We would provide the canoes, fried chicken and obligatory wine and beer. The moonlit St. Marks River would provide the magic. The whole experience would cost about a hundred bucks, but the gains made for environmental causes were immeasurable. Lawmakers are human; they like to please their friends, and by trip's end, we were often counted among their friends. So was the river and all that it represented.

One Labor Day weekend, my cousin Tom and I decided to embark on a kayaking trip on this middle section of river. We dropped my truck off at the U.S. 98 public landing at Newport and launched two kayaks at the Gluckman's house. We enjoyed a leisurely three-hour paddle.

Upon arriving at the public landing, we were shocked to find more than a hundred revelers in advanced stages of inebriation. Large sunburned men watched us with amusement. We felt like a pair of deer, with handsome racks, leisurely strolling through a hunt camp on Thanksgiving weekend.

Tom and I looked for my truck. To our chagrin, we found it nestled among trees far from our original parking spot. It was blocked in by pickups and a loud horseshoe game. The ground was littered with trash, mostly beer bottles, which angered me particularly, since I had fought unsuccessfully for a bottle bill in Florida.

One young man ran up to us. "Oh, is that your truck?" he asked nervously. I nodded.

"We didn't hurt nothing," he blurted. "It was just in the way of the game." He nodded towards the wild-eyed men tossing horseshoes. By the excitement that each shot generated, I gathered that more than pride was on the line.

"How did you move the truck?" I asked, incredulous.

The man flashed a prideful smile. "About twenty of us just picked up the back end and rolled it by the front tires," he said. "It didn't hurt nothing."

I chuckled. Two bare-chested men began rolling on the ground in a drunken brawl. Their grunts were momentarily drowned out by screeching brakes and blaring horns from the bridge area as someone tried to pull out in front of oncoming traffic.

"You mind helping me get the truck out?" I asked, nonchalant.

"Yeah, no problem."

With the helpful man directing traffic and getting friends to move trucks, we managed to avoid thick mud, flying horseshoes, the brawlers, and a massive guy who swayed back-and-forth but stood his ground; he taunted us to run him over.

On another occasion, this time on a weekday, I visited the Newport Bridge to find a man who was seeking crewmates to raft with him to the Texas coast. Friends had stimulated my curiosity, describing how the man sought to re-enact the voyage of Spanish conquistadors who built makeshift rafts near the mouth of the St. Marks River to escape hostile Apalachee Indians in 1528. The desperate Spaniards created a bellows out of deer hides and forged nails and tools out of weapons, spurs, and stirrups. They felled towering pines and shaped oars from junipers. They crafted sails from clothing, water bags from horse skin, and ropes and rigging from palmetto husks and horsehair. In the end, they had constructed five primitive sailing rafts for 242 men. Cabeza de Vaca, one of four survivors of the journey, wrote a journal of his ordeal, a journal that had evidently inspired the man beneath the bridge.

After parking at Ouzt's Oyster Bar on the west side of the river, I walked toward the bridge and approached a stocky, sunburned man sewing together a crude sail. He sat on a long raft made of pine logs. A pot of a black, tar-like substance smoldered on a smoky fire nearby. I don't remember the man's name, so I shall call him Cabo.

Cabo glanced up and brushed stringy brown hair from his sweat-stained face. I deduced that his dark eyes revealed Spanish heritage. I asked him about his project. Cabo sighed, slurped a Budweiser, checked on the smoldering substance of what I assumed to be pitch for waterproofing lashings and logs, and began his story.

Like Cabeza de Vaca, Cabo planned to sail to the Texas coast, and then walk inland for several hundred miles to Mexico City, often through desert terrain. De Vaca, he said, had been a messiah. "He healed people," he asserted. "He made his way to Mexico City by healing the Indians he met. Many Indians started following him."

Cabo admitted two main problems with his plan. He had no sailing experience, and he needed a crew--not the nearly fifty men who squeezed onto de Vaca's raft. Three or four would suffice, enough to help launch and guide the boat and man the sails. "You interested?" he asked.

I glanced skeptically at the stick lean-to Cabo had built on the deck. Not exactly the Love Boat, I thought. I had been prone to crazy adventures in the past, but sailing a makeshift raft along the Gulf Coast with no motor or running lights seemed an invitation to disaster. There was a reason why the would-be Spanish conquerors of 1528 lost four out of five rafts and 238 men. Any number of misfortunes could doom the journey, storms and large ships at night being among them. Plus, Cabo's raft looked heavy. The logs weren't seasoned. I feared it would sink soon after launching.

"My wife would kill me," I finally answered.

A few weeks later, I visited the Newport Bridge again. Cabo was gone. So was his raft. I heard later that, unable to find a crew, he abandoned his efforts. The raft lies at the bottom of the St. Marks, the newest addition to the river's storehouse of historical memorabilia.

Below Highway 98, the St. Marks wends its way past oil refineries, seafood restaurants, bars, and a bed and breakfast in the town of St. Marks, and then it gets wild again—abruptly—merging with the spring-fed Wakulla River at the ruins of Fort San Marcos. For almost three hundred years, the fort was at the center of a tug-of-war between Native Americans, Europeans, pirates and Americans vying for control of North Florida. Now it is a peaceful tree-covered spot, contrasting its long and often violent history. Nature's recuperative powers, always strong, seem to display extra vitality along the lower St. Marks River.

I often dream about the St. Marks. In one dream, I am floating down the river, the new leaves of spring casting bright green reflections on tannic waters. Birds speak to me, and fish, otters, and manatee. The river herself communicates—a whisper, an understanding. I begin to see those who have gone before: Apalachee, conquistadors, the Spanish fort, Civil War combatants and abandoned river towns such as Port Leon and Magnolia. The St. Marks has absorbed them all, and each year new leaves sprout, the mullet run, manatees return, and colorful warblers fill the trees.

The river keeps on flowing.

If You Go

The St. Marks River can be accessed at a couple of locations. You can paddle upstream from a primitive landing at Natural Bridge Battlefield Historic State Park, about five miles east of Woodville on Natural Bridge Road. The current is moderate and the river passable, although log strainers may be present, especially during dry periods.

There is no public access directly below Natural Bridge where the river emerges again from underground at the St. Marks River Rise Spring. To paddle this segment, you can launch at the Newport Bridge ramp (northeast side) along Highway 98 and paddle upstream. It is six miles to the St. Marks River Rise Spring, making for a 12 mile round trip paddle. The river shoreline is largely undeveloped. Some area outfitters, such as the Wilderness Way (850-877-7200) and TNT Hideaway (850-925-6412), lead guided trips from a private launch just below St. Marks River Rise Spring to the Newport Bridge, making for a six mile paddle with the current.

Below the Newport Bridge, it is an easy 4.5 mile paddle through the town of St. Marks to a launch area at the San Marcos de Apalache Historic State Park.

Wild pig along the St. Marks River near Newport.

Kayaks along the lower Ocklawaha River.

11
Rawlings Country

"South of Otter Landing the river bluffs flattened, and scrub met swamp in a twisting moil of briers and rattan and moccasins. There was no fertile ledge of hammock. Only cypresses reared their feathery heads from gigantic bases."
--Marjorie Kinnan Rawlings, *South Moon Under*, 1933

Florida is largely a state of transplants, and many newcomers know little about their adopted home, while having a tremendous environmental impact. That's why it's refreshing to find people who seem to wear old Florida on their sleeve, who snugly fit into the land like a perfectly-sized shoe.

Florida natives David and Becky Ziegler live in a chunk of north-central Florida known as the Big Scrub, a unique land wedged between the St. John's and Ocklawaha rivers, and marked by almost 600 lakes and ponds and crystal spring runs well known to paddlers— Juniper Creek, Salt Springs Run and Alexander Springs Creek.

Walking through the sandy scrub near their home, it can seem like a parched jungle, and nearly impenetrable. Thick myrtle oak, saw-toothed palmetto and huge teardrop-shaped Florida rosemary impede movement. If looking up, spindly sand pines dominate the view. They lean and twist in a scattergun pattern as if placed there by a tornado. It is easy to become lost, and, minus a compass or global positioning system, one hopes for a river, lake or more open stand of longleaf pine forest or hardwood hammock to gain bearings.

A century ago, the scrub was viewed by proper society as marginal land with poor soils and God-forsaken environments. The people who came to live there were viewed as marginal as well.

In the 1930s, noted author Marjorie Kinnan Rawlings chronicled the lives of scrub residents in her novels *The Yearling* and *South Moon Rising*. *The Yearling*, about a hardscrabble pioneer boy raising a fawn, won Rawlings national acclaim and the Pulitzer Prize for fiction.

The people described by Rawlings were a colorful, independent breed who eked out a living by farming, hunting, fishing and peddling moonshine. Some of their descendents, like David and Becky, still carry on a lifestyle reminiscent of their forebears, minus the moonshining.

Becky Ziegler is proud of her Creek Indian heritage.

David and Becky's two-story wood house stands in full view of Lake Delancy, surrounded by family members and the vast Ocala National Forest. Originally a rustic hunting cabin, years of home improvements have included electricity, air conditioning, major appliances and modern plumbing. Their diet is what separates David and Becky from most Floridians, and the fact they live almost two miles down a tortuous sand road.

"About ninety-five percent of our meat comes from the woods and rivers and lakes," Becky told me as I sat around her curved kitchen counter. "We hunt deer and squirrels, we catch crabs, shrimp and fish, and we take home road kills if they're fresh. Armadillo is good if it's not too flat."

Buzzards are frequently deprived of food along Highway 19.

Becky's dark hair, eyes and skin are reminiscent of her Creek Indian ancestors, a heritage she proudly embraces. Several of her kinfolk live nearby on land originally obtained in the 1920s by Becky's grandfather, Pearl Guy Crews. Crews was a state legislator with an eighth grade education. He studied for the bar exam while riding in trains that took bodies of cholera victims to remote graveyards to minimize spreading the disease. He ultimately passed the exam but often joked in later years that he had to hire someone to shake his desk so it would be like writing on the train.

Crews' original house sits about a hundred yards from David and Becky's and is occupied by one of their aunts. It's where Marjorie Kinnan Rawlings used to frequently stay and write.

"This was an every weekend, every holiday, and every hunting season place all the time I was growing up," said Becky. "Being a Navy brat and moving all over the place, this was the only place that was consistent." She moved full time to the lake in 1972, and David joined her in 1990, although he had been a long-time family friend.

David Ziegler feels at home on the water.

David, a tall man with long graying brown hair and bushy beard, is a self-described "river rat." He grew up on the St. Johns River near Palatka, the closest town of any size to their woods retreat. "My daddy and my grandfather and a couple of uncles came down from Georgia in the 1930s and lived on the river to harvest coon and beaver pelts and to catch fish. Mama and Daddy lived in a tent on the river for the first three-and-a-half years of their marriage."

David described an upbringing that included harvesting and consuming nearly anything that "didn't eat me first." Survival was paramount; the law was secondary. "We even ate sea turtle and manatee," he said. "Manatee meat tastes like pork."

He even described a fish harvesting method known as "monkey fishing" whereupon fish such as catfish are shocked with a small generator attached to a car battery with two wires in the water. Early forms of the device were hand-cranked, like an early organ grinder used by a performing monkey, thus the name. Once shocked, slick-skinned fish such as catfish floated to the surface and were easily scooped up. "We'd stash the generator underneath a bridge before we got back to the landing so we wouldn't get caught," he said.

Rawlings commented on the illegal activities of Big Scrub people she encountered: "They are living an entirely natural, and very hard, life, disturbing no one," she wrote in 1931. "Yet almost everything they do is illegal. And everything they do is necessary to sustain life in that place."

During my visit, I never joined David in any illegal activities as did Rawlings when she helped a Big Scrub family dynamite mullet, shoot limpkin and stalk deer at night with a light, out of season. Today, David adheres to the law because he has witnessed first-hand the decline of many species. He and Becky have conformed their lifestyles to actively follow legally established hunting and fishing seasons.

"Bow season starts in September; gun season starts in early November and lasts till the first weekend in January; squirrel season stays open till about the first week in March," David said. "There's gobbler season in April in the forest. We fish year-round—freshwater and saltwater. Crabbing starts in April and lasts until maybe August. We catch shrimp out of the St. John's in August or September. They start running in June or the first part of July, but they're real small. We don't go until August or September when they get big." He can describe the flavor of most any fish, from gar to bowfin (mud fish), and most any game animal, from deer to raccoon.

Although mercury contamination from coal-fired power plants, incinerators and other industrial sources worries them, the Zeiglers believe that wild game, fish and shellfish are healthier than store-bought meat. "A lot of our diseases and problems are coming from this mass production of meat," said Becky. "We just don't trust the growth hormones, antibiotics and other things they give the animals."

David's "river rat" childhood helped him to survive later challenges. In 1968, he joined the Marines "and didn't know there was a war going on." Boot camp was a shock, mainly due to his first exposure to city kids. "Half the people in my boot camp didn't know how to swim. I never met anybody who didn't know how to swim," he said.

David soon found himself in a different kind of jungle where he had to fully utilize his wilderness survival skills. "It wasn't no camping trip," he said "A helicopter would drop us off in the jungle and it would take up to two months to walk back. You wore one pair of pants and they wouldn't give you another one until it rotted off your body."

After Vietnam, the forests, rivers and lakes of the Big Scrub helped David heal physical and psychological war wounds. "This was a relaxing place to come," he said. "Nobody's out here bothering you, especially on weekdays."

David often reminds me of Penny Baxter, the lead adult male character in *The Yearling*. "Something in him was raw and tender," wrote Rawlings about Baxter, depicted as a Civil War veteran. "The touch of men was hurtful upon it, but the touch of the pines was healing."

On a weekday boat trip down the lower Ocklawaha River--an undeveloped section I would later paddle with other friends--David and Becky proudly showed me places where they had camped and fished in the past. Huge alligators and regal great blue herons seemed to greet us around every bend. Gar broke the water's surface. Osprey whistled overhead.

Along the unspoiled shoreline, wax myrtle, cedar, cypress and maple arched over the water. From the pickerel weed to the treetops, my eyes feasted on multiple shades of green, with splashes of color from blooming sweetbay, spider lily and red hibiscus.

At one point, David suddenly stopped the boat, circled around, and turned off the motor. "Do you smell it," he asked. I caught a faint whiff of rotting vegetation. "When a fish makes a bed, they fan the dirt out of the sand. The dirt comes up and makes an odor. That's where you fish."

He and Becky had both noticed the smell while in a moving motorboat, almost an ingrained instinct, it seemed. Survival in the Big Scrub.

Becky pointed out something else about river life. "Everyone on the river waves to you," she said. "It's considered impolite if you don't. Maybe people should take the tops off their cars so they could wave to each other."

Regarding this familiarity, even among strangers, David added, "When I was living in Palatka, my parents knew three out of four people there. If I did something wrong, my parents knew about it before I got home. Now I can walk through Wal-Mart or Publix or Winn-Dixie and might see only one person that I know. The town's too big; that's why I live out here now."

To a newcomer like myself, the Ocklawaha is nearly pristine and filled with wildlife, but to long-time residents like David and Becky, the Ocklawaha has changed.

"We used to catch all the bass we needed every time we came out," said David. "The water was crystal clear; you could see the bottom all the way across the river. And then in the '60s they built the barge canal and made the dam and lake; now the water ain't as clear like it used to be. The water's hot; it used to be nice and cool like spring water, but it sits up on a lake and gets hot. Now, everything below the dam [Rodman Dam] is in hot water. And it used to be that you'd come down here and there'd be white birds leaving a trail; you'd just follow the birds down the river. Don't know why they left."

Becky said the same thing about Lake Delancy. "At sunset, when I was a little girl, those islands out in the middle of the lake looked like it had snowed on them they'd be so full of white birds. Now they're gone." Many of the white birds David and Becky remember were white ibis, or curlew, once a prized food of many early scrub residents. Rawlings wrote about people hunting them. Now, they are simply appreciated for their beauty, if one is fortunate enough to see them. Like many wildlife species once taken for granted, their former abundance is sorely missed.

The Zeiglers have noticed more people on the water and in the woods, the Ocala being one of the most frequently visited national forests in the country. They point to countless new trails in the forest made by off-road vehicles, and they are constantly picking up garbage. "Every year after hunting season ends," said Becky, "we find places where people have camped and clean up the trash."

David and Becky have a vested interest in keeping their section of the Big Scrub clean. In touring me through the woods, it was obvious the open longleaf forests and thick stands of sand pine (what Rawlings called Southern spruce) are storehouses for memories, like living photograph albums. Every nook in the woods seemed to have a story to tell—a deer harvested, a human encounter, a bear sighting, an accident. "I learned how to drive in the backwoods when I was ten," said Becky. "I went all through here."

Biologists will quickly point out the uniqueness of Ocala's scrub habitat--its origin as a Pleistocene seashore and possible island; its rare forms of wildlife such as the Florida scrub lizard, sand skink, and Florida scrub-jay; its dependence on infrequent catastrophic fires to regenerate itself. But for David and Becky and many others, it's more personal than that.

Near the end of my visit, David and Becky lead me down the road from their house to meet Becky's elderly aunt, Ona Crews Williamson. With clear eyes and a strong voice, she described Big Scrub life before her family's first cabin was built on Lake Delancy. "My mother and daddy camped on the lake," she said. "They put us kids in cribs that was covered with window wire. It kept out mosquitoes and it helped to retard the panthers and bobcats from getting the kids and dragging them off. We grew up down here with panthers. They used to go in front of the camp all the time."

For self-defense, she was given a .22 rifle when she was six years old—"but you couldn't shoot anything that was alive unless it threatened you." She never needed to use the gun.

I asked her about Marjorie Kinnan Rawlings. "She was a fan of my daddy's," she began, "and I guess he was a fan of hers. She wrote part of her books down here. She'd spend months at a time down here at the big camp. She'd sit out on the screened porch and write and write by hand. She was a real nice lady, I remember."

I yearned to hear more. Marjorie Kinnan Rawlings had always been one of my favorite Florida authors, but I had never actually met someone who knew her. Becky offered to take me to the original cabin of her grand-father's. We bid our farewell to Ms. Williamson and strolled down a sunlight-dappled sand road, beneath arching live oaks draped with Spanish moss. We soon entered a tin-roofed cracker-style house perched off the ground on blocks. Becky hollered a greeting. Another of

Becky's aunts, Juanita Massey, approached and clasped my hand. She toured me through rooms adorned with deer mounts, rusted muskets, wagon wheels and kerosene lamps--real old Florida. Becky spoke for me. "Juanita, Doug wants to know more about Marjorie Kinnan Rawlings."

The woman nodded in recognition. Like Becky's other aunt, she was only a child when Ms. Rawlings used to visit, but her memories were still vivid. "She always wore no shoes and an old country cotton dress," she said. "Just real down to earth—with her feet propped up on the porch rails."

The Crews family cabin on Lake Delancy.

Becky took me to the back porch and urged me to sit in one of the original vintage rockers that faced the lake. I didn't need much urging. Sighing, I placed my feet on the long foot rail, polished and dark from the oils of countless feet, including those of Ms. Rawlings. Outside, two sandhill cranes poked about the grass before a vast body of sparkling water that was Lake Delancy. "When can I move in?" I asked.

My kind hosts chuckled, understanding. For a brief moment, the Big Scrub was whole again. Panthers still roamed. Dams had never been built across wild rivers. Brilliant white curlews filled surrounding trees, electrifying the air with angel-like wings.

And from the far end of the yard, a barefoot boy emerged, running alongside a nimble fawn. Sunlight beamed off his radiant cheeks. He was pure, alive, embodying the spirit of Original Florida. My eyes followed his bounding steps until streams from a passing jet separated the sky.

If You Go

Paddlers in Putnam County have put together an extensive network of paddling trails called the Putnam County Blueways. The trails include part of the St. Johns River, the lower Ocklawaha River, Crescent Lake, and various smaller streams. Ocala National Forest paddling trails are described on the Florida Paddling Trails Association website: www.floridapaddlingtrails.com.

12
Wild Rivers, Limpkins and the Mall

It was a classic modern conflict. My then teenage daughter and I both had a day off, she from school and I from work, and we wanted to spend it together. But she wanted to go to a mall; I wanted to canoe a wild river and photograph wading birds. Irreconcilable differences? No, we simply agreed to do both.

On the morning of the outing, I pulled Cheyenne out of bed after frequent wake-up attempts and cajoled her into helping me load the canoe onto our vehicle. I appreciated the fact that she was now strong enough to help me with such tasks.

During the 20-minute drive to the Wacissa River just east of Tallahassee, Cheyenne asked an all too typical question: "Can I change the station?" My oldies radio station was, well, "too old." The easy listening one—"too slow." The news station—"too boring." I grimaced when the contemporary pop/hip-hop station was chosen. I have determined that some aspects of fatherhood involve an occasional suspension of sanity in order to obtain peace in the household. After all, our children are only with us for a short time. I was still relieved when we were finally floating on the water, sans man-made noise that sometimes passes off as music, and enjoying a wide river panorama.

Great blue heron along the Wacissa.

Quietly cruising along a shore of thick trees, shrubs and protruding logs, it was easy to pick out snowy egrets, white ibis and tri-colored herons against a green backdrop.

Yellow-crowned night herons, green herons and little blue herons were more difficult to spot. A great blue heron seemed to pose for us as we floated to within thirty feet. At first it stood stock-still, and then it began preening as if to show that our presence was being tolerated.

Setting up a tripod in a canoe to take good bird photos was certainly a challenge, but it enabled me to keep the camera still as long as I parked the boat on a thick floating mat of hydrilla. It was one of the few advantages I could see for the pesky waterweed that is clogging many Florida waterways, including the Wacissa. Having Cheyenne to hold the boat steady with her paddle also helped. She was the ideal companion for wildlife watching—quiet, cooperative and maybe even interested. Plus, the coming mall trip was an extra incentive. No matter what you call it, "positive reinforcement" or "incentives," parenthood involves liberal doses of bribery and compromise stirred into a batter of love.

We proceeded downriver at an ultra slow pace. No matter how quiet we tried to paddle, Suwannee cooters plopped off logs well ahead of our arrival. Little blue herons squawked their alarms. Raspy hawk cries and the high-pitched laughs of pileated woodpeckers punctuated the air. I spotted a limpkin moving into the trees, but Cheyenne missed it. "The limpkin is one of the more uncommon birds in north Florida," I said, trying to impress upon her the uniqueness of the experience that she missed. "Maybe we'll see another one." We surveyed an array of empty apple snail shells that lay around the log where the limpkin had been feeding. Cheyenne picked out a shiny brown one to keep that matched the color of limpkin feathers but without the white flecks.

Limpkins have all but disappeared on the nearby Wakulla River. Biologists speculate that either thick hydrilla growth, spurred by high nitrogen levels in the water, or flooding that submerged their salmon-colored eggs on tree trunks and cypress knees, prevented apple snails from reproducing. The Wacissa must be taking up the slack because I had spotted several of the large wading birds on a recent outing. They are also coming back because they are protected. People once hunted them for food along the river, especially during the Great Depression, but not any more.

Cheyenne's interest was heightened enough to turn our outing into a quest to find a limpkin. Still, there were plenty of other sights. Cheyenne pointed out a banded water snake wriggling past the boat. An osprey whistled as it soared overhead. Cicadas whirred. Frogs bellowed. I searched for the swallow-tailed kites that I had often seen along the river—six in one group on a previous outing—but saw none of the quiet and graceful raptors. Also, after another mile, no limpkins. I silently asked for a bit of cooperation from Mother Nature. After all, I had a teenager to impress, one who was saturated with pop music, mall shopping, contemporary Hollywood flicks, electronic games, schoolwork and all of the social accouterments of high school life. There were also driving lessons and the eventual discussions about buying her a car. Canoeing the Wacissa was a natural, and inexpensive, addition to a teenage world still being shaped.

We stopped for a swim at Big Blue, a 45-foot-deep spring along a riverside creek. It is one of twelve known springs scattered along the upper mile-and-a-half of the river. We met four people from England who were seeing a bit of "wild America." They were enthralled by the river but were dismayed that the normally clear spring was murky due to recent rains.

Alligator lifeguard at Big Blue Spring.

I usually meet local residents at Big Blue. On occasion, a rope swing is present and I have often watched daredevils take Tarzan-like swings into the spring. Unlike other area swimming holes, Big Blue is surprisingly free of trash. "It's the locals who keep this place clean," one man had explained to me. "We take care of the river."

One recent change along the Wacissa that elicited mixed reactions from local residents was the purchase of extensive tracts of riverfront property for preservation by the state of Florida. Folks can become nervous about any kind of change, especially one put forward by the government, but an onslaught of riverfront homes and docks would not be welcome either. State officials assured river users that opportunities would remain for hunting, fishing, swinging from trees and for photographing wading birds.

Leaving Big Blue, I was delighted to hear a loud clucking type sound. "I think that's a limpkin," I whispered to Cheyenne. "Let's just drift around the bend and see if we can find it." Closely related to rails and cranes, limpkins are also known as "the crying bird" for their eerie mournful cries, but we just heard a *kr-ow, kr-ow, kr-ow*. Nearly hidden behind tall spires of wild rice, we spotted the limpkin. It was feeding on an apple snail alongside a weathered log. After finishing the treat, it began to bob its head and neck up and down in a strange kind of dance while doing its clucking sound. This halting type of gait reminded early observers of someone walking with a limp, thus the name "limpkin."

From deep within the floodplain forest, we heard an answering *kr-ow* from an unseen limpkin. A duet was soon established with the visible limpkin. "This is incredible," I whispered. "I've never witnessed limpkins communicating to each other before. Very few people do."

Cheyenne nodded, appearing impressed. Perhaps she wouldn't blow off the mall entirely (limpkins aren't THAT mesmerizing), but in the long run, I knew this experience would be more memorable.

Most of my previous limpkin encounters had been on the river boat cruise at Wakulla Springs State Park. Along with very healthy looking alligators, limpkins were a highlight of the tour, a feature that is now sorely missed by park personnel and visitors. The disappearance of any native animal that has inhabited a place for millennia is often seen as a bellwether of future troubles. The limpkin is a "species of special concern" in Florida for good reason.

Eventually, the limpkin we were watching retreated toward its companion in the floodplain forest and so we began paddling our way back upriver. We watched a mother wood duck escort her ducklings across the river, frequently calling to a straggler in the brood. That elicited an excited response from Cheyenne. Baby ducks, covered in downy feathers, are enough to melt any young person's heart. It was all part of the Wacissa's magic, the magic of a wild river.

A limpkin and turtle share a log on the Wacissa River.

We docked the boat just as rain began to fall. I quickly shuttled my camera and gear to the car. The rain paused in time for us to load the canoe. It also allowed me to say a silent goodbye to the Wacissa, a river utilized by humans for more than 12,000 years and never tamed. Even its name is so old that its meaning has been lost, buried with the early Apalachee Indians and Spaniards.

Soon, I would enter a domain where wildness is forbidden—a mall. Still, I vowed to take part of the river with me in thoughts and dreams.

Later, when I closed my eyes, I hoped to envision the patriarchal great blue heron that perches across from the main headwater springs, and the more secretive limpkins bobbing and poking into waterweeds, perhaps not knowing the small but special niche they filled in a father's relationship with his daughter.

Guidelines for Taking Young People to Wild Places

--Know the age group and be flexible. With younger children it is best to plan "adventures" and "explorations." But, remember, excursions can be more fulfilling if there is less focus on getting from point A to point B and more on what can be discovered in between.
--Bring company. When my daughter was younger, I marveled at how she could walk for miles without complaint if an interested friend was along.
--Bring an expert. An animal tracker, wild food identifier, sportswoman, birds, etc., can spark additional interest.
--Take accessories. Binoculars, scopes, swimming masks, magnifying lenses, cameras, field guides, all can add quality to an outing.
--Bring snacks and drinks. Take treats that are not normally eaten at home.
--Take your time. Children are naturally inquisitive. That curiosity alone can often lead an outing.
--Include the arts. Combine the outing with activities such as painting, drawing, poetry, photography and storytelling.
--Leave electronic devices at home or turn them off. This should be for young people and adults alike.

If You Go

The upper Wacissa River can easily be accessed from Highway 27 between Tallahassee and Perry. At the Highway 59 junction, head south four miles to the four-way stop in the town of Wacissa. Keep driving south about a mile. When Highway 59 forks to the right, keep going straight until the road dead-ends at one of the Wacissa River headsprings.

The upper Wacissa is an easy river to paddle upstream or downstream. Weekends can be busy and an occasional airboat can shatter the quietness of the experience. Two local outfitters near the headsprings rent kayaks and canoes.

The unmistakable silhouettes of swallowtail kites can often be seen along the Wacissa in spring and summer.

13
Rally for the Wacissa

"We never know the worth of water till the well is dry."
--Thomas Fuller, *Gnomologia*, 1732

History was made on a November afternoon in 2010 at the Wacissa River headsprings. More than 200 residents from the tiny town of Wacissa and folks from outlying communities and the city of Tallahassee gathered to show support for this clear, spring fed river in the wake of Swiss giant Nestle's plan to withdraw hundreds of thousands of gallons a day from the Wacissa watershed. The rally participants drove compact cars and pickups, set up tents and grills and freely shared food, and they brought their watercraft—airboats, pontoon boats, bass boats, canoes, kayaks... Never before had so diverse a coalition rallied around the river.

Friendships were formed on that crisp clear day that was never deemed possible only a short time before, and there were several firsts. Paddlers embarked on chilly airboat rides, while boaters tested their balance on stand-up paddleboards. Young and old alike hand-drew signs of protest and expressed their love for the river. And whether they were four years old or eighty, it was obvious that the Wacissa River had gotten into their blood. Many had spent their entire lives fishing and swimming, boating and paddling, in and on these pristine waters. And to risk any of it for the profits of a few was too much to bear.

The "Kumbaya" atmosphere hasn't always been the case on the Wacissa. Paddlers have long complained about the loud airplane-like noise of airboats while airboaters and other boaters tire of seeing kayaks and canoes blanket the river channel. And legally, boaters can't regard paddlecraft as simply speed bumps, so an uneasy tolerance has developed. That is, until Nestle Waters arrived. The diverse opposition became unified and handshakes and backslaps became the norm instead of half-hearted waves on the water or the cupping of hands over ears.

Kent Koptiuch of Nestle boldly showed up at the rally to explain why his company was paying a nearby landowner to sink several test wells. Nestle's goal was to tap into a conduit for one of the river's many headsprings in order to fill sixty to seventy tanker trucks a day for indeterminate periods to deliver water forty miles to a bottling plant in Madison, Florida. It is part of their broadening effort to find new spring sources for their well known bottled water lines such as Deer Park, Zephyr Hills, Arrowhead and Poland. Koptiuch maintained that the area around the wells will be protected and that pumping will occur only after approval by the Suwannee River Water Management District. Even though no jobs would be provided by the pumping, Koptiuch said the company would address the area's substandard roads as well as improve public river access. Most in the crowd weren't buying it. "Just go home," yelled one woman, "we don't need you here and we don't want you!"

Sixty-five year old Wacissa resident Roland Brumbley summed up Nestle's arguments with a homespun saying from his family, "You can't pee in my ear and say that it's raining."

Others vowed to boycott bottled water, citing not only its impact on water resources, but its consumption of energy and contribution to the plastic waste stream. Most springs experts, such as former Florida Springs Ambassador Jim Stevenson, maintained that not enough is known about the potential impacts of pumping on the Wacissa watershed. Studies could take years, and if the Nestle pumping is approved in the interim by the Jefferson County Commission and the Suwannee River Water Management District, it may be too late for remedial steps. Plus, one large commercial well could lead to others.

A Nestle attempt to withdraw water from Lilly Springs on the Santa Fe River was defeated in 2010 amid worries that the flow of the springs and the river would be diminished. Increased truck traffic on area roads was another concern. Similar proposals in Maine and California also met the same fate. But that hasn't deterred Nestle. With an army of well paid lawyers, scientists and public relations representatives, they spread out across North America in search of primary and satellite water sources.

Many who attended the historic Wacissa rally felt like I did. I had visited the river for more than forty years and had never been disappointed. There was always enough water to paddle a kayak or canoe and the birds, fish and other wildlife were incomparable. The beauty of the clear water and springs, old growth cypress and other shoreline trees often gave me the feeling that little has changed on the river since Native Americans plied these waters in dugout canoes. So now the Wacissa River needed help. It was time to give back.

To become involved with the effort, log onto: www.savethewacissa.com.

14
Paddling Florida's Turtle River

"The vegetation is so thick and the scene so wild that it seems we are on the Congo instead of the Loxahatchee."
--Harold C. Rolls, *Palm Beach Post*, 1923

My only mistake in paddling the Loxahatchee River on a Tuesday was in failing to check with the outfitter first. They were closed. That meant not having a shuttle, and that meant paddling the river down and up and then up and down in two halves, adding considerably more miles than the 8.5 listed in the guide. The trade-off was that I had the river to myself, and what a river! The Loxahatchee was not designated Florida's first national wild and scenic river in 1985 for being lined with houses. The winding yellow-black water traverses one of southeast Florida's wildest domains: the 11,500-acre Jonathan Dickinson State Park.

Soon after embarking from Palm Beach County's scenic River Bend Park, I paddled beneath a canopy of old-growth cypress trees mixed with arching palms. Leathery ferns towered over my kayak. Crying kingfishers darted in and out of openings and the raps of woodpeckers and occasional squawks of herons pierced the air. Around most bends, turtles sunned themselves on logs, their legs splayed out to help them cool their bodies. These are the creatures that inspired Seminole Indians to give the river its name, although the proper Seminole name was *Loh-juh Hatchee*, or Turtle River. Pronunciation of many Seminole place names have been corrupted over time. But with regard to the Loxahatchee, the Seminoles could also have named it the *Hul-bah-duh Hatchee*—Alligator River. On more than one narrow bend, I brushed close to one of the sunning beasts whose length and girth matched my ten-and-half foot kayak. No aggression was displayed among either party, however.

According to the late Seminole leader Betty Mae Jumper, in her autobiography *A Seminole Legend*, the Loxahatchee River did bear a different name at one time. During the Second Seminole War, Jumper's ancestors were camped on the Loxahatchee River thinking that a peace agreement was still in place—The Macomb Treaty. "One day when most of the men were out hunting, soldiers suddenly came and surrounded a camp of Seminoles, mostly old men, women, and children, along a river," she wrote. "That is why the river there was from that day on called 'Lo-tsa-hatchee,' meaning 'River of Lies' in Creek, because our people thought that peace had been made. The soldiers gathered the Indians like criminals, making them all sit down in the open fields. Some were lucky enough to run away, and those who escaped ran to other camps to warn them." The name *Lo-tsa-hatchee* was later changed to Loxahatchee, River of Turtles.

The last major battle of the Second Seminole War battle also occurred along the shores of the swampy stream. Major General Thomas Jesup encountered a group of Seminoles in late January of 1838. A fierce battle was fought as Seminole warriors held off Jesup's superior force long enough for their families to retreat. Then, like so many other Seminole war battles, the warriors stealthily vanished into the vast swamps.

Fortunately, the Loxahatchee is peaceful now, only battered by the occasional hurricane. The narrow upper river is maintained by the Canoe Outfitters, based at River Bend Park. Otherwise, frequent snags would be challenging. As it is, a three or four foot section is usually cut out of a snag or log, allowing passage for the paddler. No motorboats are allowed in the upper river and very few boats except for kayaks and canoes could navigate the twisting channel anyhow. Plus, two small log dams or weirs require portaging. You can hear the falling water long before reaching the structures. The dams were originally constructed in the 1930s by local families to maintain water levels for farm irrigation and they are maintained primarily for historical purposes. Being rather rustic in appearance, they seem to fit in with the river's wild nature. Plus, they help keep water levels high enough for paddling. Wood drag-over ramps make for easy portaging around the dams.

Despite man's best efforts, nature can still block the Loxahatchee channel. In 2004 and 2005, three hurricanes effectively closed the river to paddlers for almost six months until crews could clear a path. During dry months, usually from February to early summer, some portaging in the river channel is generally necessary due to low water.

Roughly the mid-point on the paddling trail is Trapper Nelson's homestead, a state park interpretive site. This also marks the point where the Loxahatchee widens and becomes a mangrove-lined estuary. Tides exert a strong influence.

The rustic docks at Trapper Nelson's.

Trapper Nelson, known as "the Wild Man of the Loxahatchee," settled the area in the 1930s and remained until his death in 1968. He made a living by trapping animals for pelts, selling animals to zoos and visitors, selling firewood, playing poker with visitors, and caging live critters in pens for paying customers. His concrete snake pit of live rattlesnakes was highly popular.

Trapper—muscular and tanned—would usually greet visitors shirtless with an eight or nine foot indigo snake draped over his neck. Shorts and a pith helmet completed the outfit. Trapper was quick with a smile and tall tale, and he loved to mooch food off of visitors. Tourists, celebrities, local residents and school kids all beat a path to the legendary homestead. They paid an entrance fee of fifty cents for adults and a quarter for children. People could also rent one of the rustic guest cabins and freely use the stout rope swing over the river. "It may be hard for some people today to envision, but back then, to all these northerners, the Loxahatchee was just as exciting as going up the Amazon," said Nathaniel Reed in *Life and Death on the Loxahatchee: The Story of Trapper Nelson* by James Snyder. "You expected to see Tarzan just around the corner—only in this case, there he was!"

Trapper did use banks, especially since he bought and sold land along the river, but the park service found a hidden cache of silver coins several years after they acquired the site, most likely from entrance fees to his zoo.

To tour the trapper's homestead is to tour a piece of Old Florida, harkening back to an era not that long ago when most of Florida was wild and land was relatively cheap. The cabins and outbuildings, along with the dock and boardwalk, have all been hewn by hand, primarily built out of old-growth cypress and pine. Tour boats visit the site every two hours from four miles downstream in the state park, but I was fortunate in that low tide prevented the boat from reaching the interpretive site in mid-afternoon. I had the place to myself, par for the course on this day. So, I hung out at Trapper Nelson's until his old cabins and sheds cast long shadows; then I returned to paddling the river of turtles.

If You Go

The Palm Beach County Riverbend Park near Jupiter can easily be reached by taking the Florida Turnpike or I-95 and turning west onto State Road 706 and traveling 1.5 miles. To reach Jonathan Dickinson State Park, follow signs from exit 87A off I-95 or exit 116 off the Florida Turnpike. For a map and more information about paddling the Loxahatchee River, log onto http://www.dep.state.fl.us/gwt/guide/designated_paddle/Lox_guide.pdf.

These outfitters lead trips or rent canoes and kayaks on the river: the Canoe Outfitters of Florida at Riverbend Park, 1-888-272-1257; the Jupiter Outdoor Center, 561-747-0063; and the Loxahatchee River Adventures in Jonathan Dickinson State Park, 772-546-2771.

15
The Almost Famous Graham Creek

"I never leaf through a copy of *National Geographic* without realizing how lucky we are to live in a society where it is traditional to wear clothes."
--Irma Bombeck

"I remember when an editor at the *National Geographic* promised to run about a dozen of my landscape pictures from a story on the John Muir Trail as an essay, but when the group of editors got together, someone said that my pictures looked like postcards.
--Galen Rowell

*N*ational Geographic. The name drew our attention. A photographer who claimed to be on assignment for one of the famous magazine's spinoff publications,

National Geographic Adventure, had called my friend
Georgia, co-owner of a local outfitter. He said he needed
subjects in kayaks to pose for him on a creek or river near
the Forgotten Coast and Tate's Hell for an upcoming
feature. No money was offered. Georgia gladly obliged
pro-bono since it was a chance to highlight eco-tourism
opportunities in our area and possibly boost business.
Georgia contacted a couple of friends, including me, and a
trip was planned.

I suggested a scenic tupelo gum- and cypress- lined
creek just north of Apalachicola Bay: Graham Creek. It
was wild and remote, completely contained in protected
state lands. The photographer was driving in from central
Florida and would meet us there. "The earlier the better,"
he told me over the phone, "to take advantage of good
lighting."

At Georgia's shop around sunrise on a crisp fall
Sunday, five starry-eyed kayakers loaded up boats onto
Georgia's truck, including a stable sit-on-top variety for
the photographer. I was joined by my wife Cyndi. "I
wonder who's going to make it in the magazine," one of
the kayakers wondered aloud.

"Maybe all of us," I said hopefully. Everyone wore
bright colors, except Cyndi and me. That, I realized, might
bump the two of us from consideration.

There's something about *National Geographic*, the
official journal of the National Geographic Society since
1888, which gets people's attention. The fact that *National
Geographic Adventure* is a relatively new offshoot of the
original publication didn't matter. It still carried the
lineage of magazine royalty.

I've been to estate sales where people had kept
nearly every issue of *National Geographic* since the

1920s. Mildewed stacks stood in a closet, sorted by decades. People simply had trouble pitching or recycling them. I for one had kept prized issues for more than twenty years, while nearly all other magazines of the era had long been donated or recycled. Geographic's articles were always well researched, albeit written and edited in a rather formulaic style. But it was the photography that often compelled my interest. Only the best photographs graced the pages of *National Geographic*, the cream of the cream. So we were understandably excited that our images could find immortality in an upcoming issue. *National Geographic*… It's not just your grandfather's magazine.

My cell phone rang. It was the photographer. He was already at the Graham Creek ramp, having arrived well before our planned nine o-clock meet-up time. "Smoke on the water," he said excitedly, referring to fog rising over the water at first light. He had driven half the night to get there. He seemed impatient.

"We're strapping on the boats now," I told him, "but it will take us an hour-and-a-half to get there." Graham Creek was about eighty miles southwest of Tallahassee. The fastest way to reach it was to drive Highway 20 to Hosford, then drive forty or so miles south on the remote Highway 65. I suddenly felt guilty that we hadn't loaded up the kayaks in the wee hours and launched before sunrise.

The photographer was snoozing in his truck when we arrived at the landing. He stirred awake when we pulled up and we made hasty introductions. "The magazine wants a full page kayaking photo," he explained while we loosened the boat straps, "so one or more of you will make it, but I can't make any promises about who it will be."

"Fair enough," I responded. It was a bit like a raffle, except our individual odds were twenty percent or better of winning.

Quickly launching before the soft morning light faded, we paddled east toward the creek's headwaters. The waterway gradually narrowed through a maze of cypress and Ogeechee tupelo trees with their huge swollen bases and myriad trunks. Some were storm-battered and scarred by lightning, but still alive. Thick overhead branches soon created an interlocking canopy. With the still, coffee-colored water, it was like paddling through a mirror.

Old growth, twisted cypress tree off Graham Creek.

The photographer seemed satisfied with the setting. How could he not be? He set up a shot along a bend and had us take turns paddling past him. If we were immature participants in a reality television show, we might have pushed another person's kayak into a tree, or tipped someone over, but we were friendly and supportive like the public persona of *American Idol* contestants.

The photographer keyed on the youngest member of our group; she had a pretty smile. He didn't care for the clothes that Cyndi and I wore—they were comfortable and outdoors looking, but not the "Columbia" brand image he sought. And to one member of our group, he commented, "Do you know that you squint when you smile. No matter how many shots I've taken, you're still squinting." He played back the shots on his digital camera to prove it. She seemed deflated. According to my calculations, that left only two survivors on the island.

Over lunch back at the ramp, one in which the photographer munched on home-made quiche offered by our group, he pridefully gave us a slide show of his work on his laptop. There were some great shots. He rattled off publications where his photos had been featured. Did I mention that his ego was also on display? "Don't worry," he told us, "even if some of you don't make it in the magazine, I'll send each of you a high resolution photo of yourself. It's the least I can do to show my appreciation for you volunteering to help me out." Everyone gave him personal e-mail addresses. He seemed friendly and sincere.

After the midday break, there was more posing and shooting on a scenic fork of Graham Creek called the South Fork, even though it extends north from the creek. The afternoon light created a warmth of color. Golden cypress needles reflected on the dark mirror surface. One cypress with a huge twisted base resembled the head of a giant mastodon. No joke.

Near another picturesque tree base, the photographer began breaking off dead branches that he thought detracted from the composition. Cyndi's and my patience began wearing thin. We didn't like manipulating the environment for a few photos. While the photographer keyed on the three Columbia outfitted paddlers, Cyndi and I explored the upper reaches of the South Fork. The creek narrowed as light faded, the water an obsidian-black. There was nary a sign of people except for the occasional trot line. I took a few photos of my own. With no sounds or signs of machines, only the gentle dipping of our paddles, it seemed we were in a much earlier time.

We passed a weathered old-growth cypress that had been riddled by woodpeckers. Some of the holes had likely been made long ago by ivory-billed woodpeckers, a species that was possibly extinct today. Paddling the remote waterway, far from human hamlets, made the trip worthwhile. And then I flashed to the photographer and felt a twinge of guilt. What if this pristine creek were featured in an international magazine? Would it suddenly be overrun? Why had I agreed to be an accomplice?

It was nearly dark when our group paddled back to the ramp. The photographer said his farewells, promising again to e-mail us attachments of high caliber photos and to put in a plug for Georgia's business with the writer. While he drove away, we loaded up the kayaks and gear like good lackeys and drove home. A week passed, then two. No word from the photographer. No promised photos. Another week went by. A member of our group called me. "You hear anything?"

"Nope," I replied. "He didn't answer my last e-mail."

Georgia called soon after that. "Did you hear from that photographer?"

"Not a peep," I said. She had also sent an e-mail and received no answer.

Georgia was more tactful than I was about the situation. "I hate to say anything bad about him," she said, "only to learn later that something happened to him."

"You've got a point," I agreed. On the Internet, I saw that the photographer was teaching photography classes, so he was obviously still functioning, but I said nothing to Georgia. Sometimes it's healthier to just assume the best about people.

More time passed. I received a call from Georgia one evening. She was on her cell phone. "I'm standing here in Border's looking at the newest issue *of National Geographic Adventure* and the article on our area," she said. "There's not one kayak photo or one of Graham Creek. Nada." And no mention of her outfitting business in the article either. We felt used. The photographer's assigned photo had obviously gotten bumped for some unknown reason, and so he had moved on. We had simply been pawns in a silly game of big name photo shoot that didn't work out. And Graham Creek remained an innocuous remote waterway, little changed for centuries.

If You Go

Graham Creek is one of eleven featured paddling trails developed by the Florida Fish and Wildlife Conservation Commission (FWC) as part of the 86,000-acre Apalachicola River Wildlife and Environmental Area. The land was purchased by the state of Florida to help protect one of the most productive estuarine areas in North America, Apalachicola Bay. The area contains the largest expanse of floodplain forest in Florida. Some of the other paddling trails include waterways with intriguing names such as Whiskey George, Thank You Ma'am, Caesar and Cash. Multi-day excursions that include designated primitive backcountry campsites are also available.

Scenery varies from narrow, twisting waterways through dense cypress and tupelo canopies, such as Graham Creek, to broad, marsh-lined streams that are greatly influenced by tides. Each season yields its own rewards, from feathery cypress needles turning rust-gold in November to the brilliant blue and purple flag irises of early spring.

On a sunny day, no matter the season, there is a good likelihood of seeing wildlife, from river otters to alligators. Bald eagles frequent the area in winter months and swallowtail kites are often spotted in spring and summer. The cooler, drier months between October and April are recommended as ideal paddling times. Summer can provide an annoying dose of fresh and saltwater mosquitoes, no-see-ums and flies. Repellent is highly recommended.

Many of the paddling trails have been designed so that off-road bicycles can be used to complete a shuttle. To aid in this effort, secure bike racks have been placed at some launch sites. Before embarking, paddlers should become aware of the different hunting seasons in the area. To obtain a free guide to the nearly one hundred miles of trails that comprise the Apalachicola River WEA Paddling Trail System, call (850) 410-4951 or log onto http://myfwc.com/viewing/recreation/wmas/lead/apalachicola-river/recreation/paddling/.

Graham Creek can be reached by turning north onto Highway 65 from Highway 98 near Eastpoint and traveling about 13.5 miles to the launch at the Graham Creek Bridge. Or, you can travel 41 miles south to the bridge on Highway 65 from Hosford. The Wilderness Way at Wakulla Station, 850-877-7200, occasionally leads trips along the creek along with Journeys of St. George Island, 850-927-3831.

Elizette Velado on Graham Creek.

16
The Lake of Canoes

"It was surreal to touch something that was built by man 2,000 years before Christ walked the earth. ... This was probably a boat factory of sort in ancient times."
--Peter Gallagher, former *Seminole Indian Tribune* reporter

Lily pads fold over as a strong breeze ripples across blue water. A gently curved blue heron feather floats on the surface. Momentarily, it swings around like a canoe, stirring its lone passenger—a dragonfly.

Along a ring of marsh and sticks, anhinga and heron stretch out wings, sunning and preening. Ospreys whistle. Crows call. A bald eagle soars overhead, fish in talons.

It's a typical afternoon on a wild Florida lake, only this is no typical lake. As I paddle my kayak across the open water of Newnan's Lake near Gainesville, I am conscious of the many dugout canoes below me. Yes, canoes. When the lake dried up during the 2000 drought, more than one hundred early Native American dugout canoes were found in the lake bottom, the largest discovery of aboriginal vessels in North America. And many more were believed hidden beneath silt and muck.

Newnan's Lake may have been a manufacturing and trading spot for dugout canoes, being strategically located near the center of the state and accessible via small watercourses to the Ocklawaha River, which, in turn, connected to the larger St. Johns River. Large forests of virgin pine and cypress adjacent to the lake provided an ample supply of logs. Although the current name of the lake refers to Colonel Daniel Newnan, a Georgia militia leader who fought the Seminoles in 1812, Native Americans have long referred to the water body as *Pithlachocco*—"where canoes are made." I can humorously picture the bargaining that may have occurred in native tongue centuries ago:

A large native man swathed in deer skins puffs on a clay pipe while greeting an approaching paddler. "Paddle right up here, brave warrior. Looks like that canoe of yours has seen better days?"

"Yes, I think it has. Plus, I've spent too many days in camp of late feasting with the clan. This old boat is riding pretty low in the water."

"Well, what you need is our cypress special— longer, wider, perfect for the mature warrior's expanding girth."

"Say, that does look good, and I like that redesign of the hull."

"Yes, it's our latest and greatest. Take it for a paddle around the lake."

"How much would it set me back?"

"Well, since it's made from grade A cypress, and because I have to pay the engineers for the hull design, I can let it go for twenty-five deer skins and five alligator hides, plus your trade-in, of course."

A gasp is heard. "And I suppose it paddles itself? Fifteen deer skins and two alligator hides is the best I can do, and I'll throw in a raccoon skin."

"You drive a hard bargain, but I've got hungry mouths to feed. Throw in five more deer skins and another alligator hide, plus that shell necklace of yours, and we've got a deal."

The deal is made and another new dugout canoe is paddled into Newnan's Lake.

This kind of bartering may have gone on along Newnan's Lake for millennia. That's because carbon dating of many of the dugouts revealed ages of 500 to 5,000 years.

If Newnan's Lake was not a trading center, the large numbers of boats found in the lake bed may simply be attributed to the broad window of time that the canoes represent. "We're not used to thinking in a time frame of several thousand years," says archeologist Dan Penton. Penton noted that at boat landings where people have traditionally tied up small fishing boats, the bottoms of rivers or lakes are often littered with wooden skiffs and johnboats of previous generations. Stretch that scenario over thousands of years, and you'll likely have hundreds of sunken boats.

And what about the traditional dugout canoe? Today, only a handful of Seminoles and Miccosukees still know how to make a dugout. One of these canoe builders is Bobby Henry of Tampa. He demonstrated canoe building for several years at the Tallahassee Museum's annual Native American Heritage Festival, where I first met him. First, Bobby would roughly shape the pine or cypress log with a chainsaw, something that was formerly done with stone axes. Then, Bobby would begin chopping and burning in order to hollow out the inside. Final smoothing and shaping was done with an adz. When finished, the hull would be about three inches thick and the sides roughly an inch wide. "Chop too much, and all you have is firewood," he warned.

With the burning, he'd lay down a bed of hot coals in the hull and intensified their heat by blowing on them through a long tube. Mud packs would help keep the fire from extending too far into the sides. It was a long tedious process and Bobby rarely finished a canoe in the few days he was visiting every year. Eventually, the log would start to rot, and Bobby would begin demonstrating again on a new log.

Bobby learned the art of dugout canoe making from his father. They would search the forest for a straight cypress tree that was six or seven feet in diameter at the base and about four feet wide higher up. Ancient peoples primarily used readily available old-growth pine. Then, Bobby remembers his father girdling the tree by cutting away the bark with an axe about five feet off the ground. They would wait up to a year for the tree to die and become lighter in weight before chopping it down and cutting it to length. The laborious task of chopping and burning would then begin.

All of the canoes found in Newnan's Lake were the fire-hollowed variety, similar to others previously found in Florida. Furthermore, as pointed out in a research paper by Ryan J. Wheeler published by *American Antiquity*, the narrow beam, low sides and rounded cross-section of most Florida and Newnan's Lake canoes weren't designed to carry heavy loads as much as to access the shallow creeks and streams feeding into and out of the lake. Although somewhat unstable, the canoes were designed to be paddled swiftly by experienced paddlers. Subsistence food items and occasional trade goods were likely the main cargos carried, the dugout serving as a type of pack animal. "The canoe was a tool of central importance in an aquatic-oriented culture," wrote Wheeler. "...The canoe was not only significant for transport and subsistence activities, but may have held an archetypal role in native Florida society and cosmology."

*Early dugout canoes on display at the
Florida History Museum in Tallahassee.*

Given the thousands of lakes and streams and more than a thousand miles of coastline in Florida, and the fact that pack animals and wheeled wagons were not available before European contact, highlights the importance of the dugout canoe to early Native Americans. Wheeler also suggests that it is possible that Native Americans could have built canals around Newnan's Lake to enhance canoe transportation, similar to how canals were built by Southwest Florida's Calusa Indians.

On average, the Newnan's Lake canoes were nearly 17 feet in length, although one fragmentary canoe measured nearly 29 feet. That is possibly a record for a pre-European contact southeastern dugout canoe. A canoe paddle found in Newnan's Lake measured nearly seven feet in length, allowing the occupant to stand up while paddling. Canoe poles were also used.

"Other Florida Archaic canoes have similar shapes and sizes, suggesting that a well-developed canoe-making tradition was shared throughout much of the Florida peninsula by ca. 5,000 to 6,000 years ago," concluded Wheeler. "This correlates with the emergence of freshwater resources in the shallow lakes of the peninsula lake district, the St. Johns River, and the Florida Everglades. The reliance on canoes for communication and transport likely contributed to the development of an extensive system of canoe trails, landings, overland paths, fords, and canoe canals."

Most of the canoes found at the bottom of Newnan's Lake were fragile and degraded; excavating them would likely have caused further damage. And some were nearly destroyed by the bulldozers of commercial deadhead loggers who were pulling out sunken old-growth timbers in the lake bottom until the practice was barred.

The lake bottom is now part of the National Register of Historic Places and the canoes have been left there for posterity, so I felt proud to be able to paddle a place with such a long canoe history, and to carry on the paddling tradition.

If You Go

The Potano Paddling Trail circles the shoreline of Newnan's Lake and dips into the ancient passageway of Prairie Creek on the southwest side of the lake. The trail is named after the Potano, a Native American tribe that lived in the area through the 1600s. Numerous eagles and wading birds nest along the lake. In fact, so many eagles nest along the lake that eggs have been used to help repopulate eagles throughout the eastern United States.

For a map of the Potano Paddling Trail, log onto http://alachuaconservationtrust.org/images/gallery/general /Potano_Paddling_trail.pdf. The easiest way to access Newnan's Lake is to take Highway 26 from downtown Gainesville and drive about three miles. When the highway veers left, stay straight on County Road 329. When you reach the lake after about a mile, turn right onto County Road 329B and in just over a mile, you'll reach Palm Point City Park. You can launch here or proceed south to the Earl P. Powers County Park or Kate's Fish Camp. Another park and access point, Owens-Illinois County Park, is on the east side of the lake.

16
Kissimmee's Gem

One of Orlando's major tourism gateways is busy Highway 192 in Kissimmee. Restaurants, motels and shopping centers all line the six to eight lane road that leads to Disney World, SeaWorld and other area theme parks. It's a strange place for a paddling trail, but Shingle Creek was there first.

I met my friend Bob Mindick at the historic Steffee Landing on Shingle Creek. I missed the turn at first because a car was too close on my tail and I didn't have enough time to properly signal. So, I turned around and made my way back, a process that took almost fifteen minutes in heavy traffic.

Bob is Osceola County's public lands manager. A former education director at SeaWorld and once a ranger at Seattle's Woodland Park Zoo, Bob now assists the county in purchasing and restoring environmentally sensitive lands. I came to know him in 2007 when we were both part of a 12-day kayaking and hiking expedition through the Kissimmee Chain of Lakes and Kissimmee River. We had paddled part of Shingle Creek on the first day of the expedition but had skipped this middle section because it was impassable due to snags and exotic weeks. All that is changing now. Bob and his crew have been removing exotics and opening up the creek as part of the expansive 1,000-acre Shingle Creek Regional Park.

Shingle Creek is significant in a couple of ways. It's considered the headwaters of the Everglades, a tributary of Lake Tohopekaliga and the Kissimmee River that ultimately feeds into Lake Okeechobee and the "River of Grass." The creek is steeped in area history, and it's taking on new life.

We launched Bob's kayak and my borrowed canoe on the creek's tannin waters. The Steffee Landing once sported an airboat rental facility where tourists could pretend they were roaring through the Everglades "River of Grass," if for only a mile before having to turn around. Now, only non-motorized or electric-powered watercraft are allowed. "The birds have really come back," said Bob, nodding to a group of curved-beaked white ibis feeding in the shallows. A great blue heron lumbered past followed by a whistling osprey. Eagles, too, are commonly seen. "We can paddle downstream to where the creek narrows and becomes real wild," Bob said, "or we can paddle upstream where it becomes wider."

"Downstream sounds great," I said. Later, Bob would show me the section of creek above the landing that wasn't so wild since some of it was within sight of a large apartment complex. An old river crossing was where adventuresome youth had been trying to emulate their "Jackass" heroes by riding down a slope into the creek while tucked in a borrowed shopping cart. "It wouldn't be so bad if they pulled the cart back out," Bob said, shaking his head. "We pulled 15 carts out of the creek last month." Perhaps the ritual was a rite of passage—you can join the group only if you roll off the bank of Shingle Creek in a shopping cart. Screams welcome.

Gliding through the coffee-black waters below the landing, we passed dead and dying popcorn trees, or Chinese tallow—an exotic pest—that had been sprayed with herbicide. Large clumps of bamboo would be next. Huge expanses of exotic water weeds had recently been removed. The creek channel was now open and native vegetation along the shores had been reestablishing itself. Historic structures, too, were being restored, including an 1800's-era log cabin near the landing. The first pioneer settlement in the region was along Shingle Creek. Those early settlers cut the centuries-old cypress for shingles and other uses, thus the name "Shingle Creek." Remnants of those early structures can still be found and others may be moved to the new park from the nearby Pioneer Village.

Farther downstream, with traffic noise fading, Bob pointed out dwellings and property that had recently been purchased. "We only work with willing sellers," he said. "We want it to be a positive experience for the sellers so word spreads to their friends and neighbors."

Bob hopes to replace some of the old docks we passed with ones that will be accessible to canoes and kayaks "so people can stop and take a picnic." In all, the county acquired more than 1,000 acres through grants and matching funds. Total cost: $11 million, a bargain considering that the land fringes the once booming

Orlando area where an acre was fetching $100,000 before the real estate bubble burst. Given Florida's boom and bust history, the boom cycle will likely return again, and park users will be glad that various agencies and people had the foresight to establish a wilderness retreat in an urban setting. Partners in establishing the Shingle Creek Regional Park include Osceola County, the city of Kissimmee, the South Florida Water Management District, the Trust for Public Land and the Florida Office of Greenways and Trails. The Florida Communities Trust, funneling money from Florida Forever, funded most of the land purchases.

Beyond the last house, the creek narrowed and we were soon immersed in a vast cypress forest. Garfish rippled the surface. Turtles slid off logs. Bob searched the shoreline for otters that he knew lived in and along the creek. "This is also great habitat for moccasins," he said with pride.

We wound around tight corners with a quickening current. "This was once clogged with weeds," he said. "But now we've cleared at least a half mile or more. The pioneers and Indians used to be able to get through here, so we want to clear another half mile or so of obstructions so paddlers can reach the lower creek and Lake Toho." Once open, paddlers will be able to travel ten unimpeded miles to Lake Tohopekaliga. They would then have the option of taking out at a landing in Kissimmee or camping on the county-maintained Makinson Island. Hardy paddlers can even turn their trip into a multi-day journey through the Kissimmee chain of lakes and the Kissimmee River.

When Bob and I reached the spot where obstructions prevented us from continuing, we paused and sat quietly, listening and watching in this cypress wilderness. A woodpecker called and a kingfisher shot past.

Bob explained that this was the area where a battle took place in the Second Seminole War, near the present-day Kissimmee Airport. Wildcat, or Coacoochee, and his warriors were engaged in a running battle with General Thomas Jesup and a thousand troops when they retreated into the thick cypress swamps around Shingle Creek. "The soldiers turned back at that point," Bob said. I could see why. Swamps were an impediment to a large army, and a great advantage for stealth Seminoles. And now this swamp had become a modern refuge in the heart of an urban area. I was glad it was still here, to be enjoyed once again by paddlers as it has for millennia.

If you Go

The Shingle Creek Paddling Trail begins at Osceola County's Shingle Creek Regional Park. It will eventually end at the ramp along Lake Tohopekaliga in Kissimmee. Steffee Landing is located only two miles west of downtown Kissimmee on Highway 192 Many people enjoy paddling up and down the stream through the park. For more information about the trail, log onto http://www.osceola.org/index.cfm?lsFuses=Department/Parks/32962 or call Osceola County Parks & Recreation, 407-742-7800. The nearest outfitting service is Kissimmee Outdoor Adventures, 800-247-1309.

17
Canoe Fishing with Lucky Paul

"It has always been my private conviction that any man who pits his intelligence against a fish and loses has it coming."
--John Steinbeck

You've probably met guys like my neighbor, Paul; there is just something they do that drives fish to bite. They can catch fish when no one else is catching fish. And so when Paul and I began driving to the coast for some canoe fishing and he asked me where I wanted to fish, I wasn't worried. We would catch fish wherever we went.

We had reached the tiny town of Newport along the St. Marks River and Paul laid out the options. "Well, we can go fishing at the St. Marks Lighthouse. I always catch fish there," he said. "Or, we can go to the lower Aucilla River. I went there Saturday and did pretty well."

I thought for a moment. The turn off to the lighthouse was coming up quickly. "Those flats off the lighthouse are usually good," I said. "But I've never been fishing on the lower Aucilla. Might be nice to try a new place."

Paul kept driving on Highway 98, past the lighthouse road. New adventures are always fun.

After a dozen miles on the paved highway and then a few miles south on a graded dirt road, we reached the public boat landing on the lower Aucilla River. Morning fog enshrouded the wide river, giving people on the water a ghostly appearance. By the many trucks and trailers parked near the landing, most with Georgia tags, it was apparent that this fishing hole was no secret. "You should see it on weekends," Paul said. I was glad this was a Tuesday.

Paul, a tall wiry fellow with a perennial sun-weathered face, worked as a finish carpenter. When work slacked off, he went fishing, often during the week when the waters weren't so crowded. Paul had joined me on other adventures, such as the swamp slog through the Mud Swamp/New River Wilderness Area (see "Paddling Through Hell"), but fishing was his specialty.

A salty character wearing a sailor's cap and rubber boots greeted us at the landing as we began un-strapping the canoe from Paul's truck. "Not as many fish upriver," he said. "Not cold enough. But the trout and reds should be coming in with the tide. You might get a couple." A couple of keeper fish for the dinner table—that's what we were banking on.

After pushing off the bank, Paul suggested that we float downriver since the tide was out. I didn't argue. Paul was a renowned fisherman in our neighborhood, one with uncanny luck. At our weekly potluck dinner gatherings, he always provided recently caught broiled fish. On more than one occasion, he caught fish when I didn't catch fish, and I'd be sitting right next to him! Increasingly, I began to scrutinize his methods.

If fishing with shrimp or any live bait, Paul uses a short hook and completely covers it. He keeps the spool on the reel open and lets the fish really take it for a few seconds before setting the reel and jerking back hard to hook the fish. Paul makes his own wire leaders that he says are thinner, less visible in the water, but just as strong as the commercial ones. He ties the leader directly onto the hook so the extra metal of a snap won't spook fish. Also, for saltwater fishing, Paul generally puts out two or three lines at once: one pole with shrimp on a bobber, one with shrimp without a bobber, and one with a chunk of cut fish on a hook.

Another thing Paul does is to always use a canoe. "There are pros and cons of each kind of boat," he says, "but with a canoe [or fishing kayak], you don't have to mess with trailers, hitches, gasoline, boat permits and most boat landings are free for canoes. It's about the only kind of boat fishing that is economical." Not exactly an advertisement for the marine industry, but great for people on a budget. Add the advantage of being able to get into remote places quietly, and the canoe or kayak has many pluses. The main negatives are obvious, too—instability in rough water and not a lot of room to move around, especially for the person sitting in the stern, like I usually did. And you don't want to paddle twenty or thirty miles into the Gulf to go deep sea fishing.

After drifting a half mile or so, some fish began nibbling on our shrimp. Paul gently placed the anchor in the water and released it. In a canoe, you don't just heave the anchor overboard. Sudden movements are a no-no, for obvious reasons.

I used to go fishing by myself in a one-person canoe using a kayak paddle. It worked great. Most everything I needed was in front of me, but the most awkward part was trying to lean back far enough to drop the anchor, or to pull it up. I tried tying it near the middle of the canoe once to make it easier; it met with disastrous results. The wind was blowing hard and having the wind hit me broadside in such a small canoe nearly tipped me over, especially when I started pulling up the anchor. In wind, anchors for canoes need to be in the stern or bow—or else.

Being more stationary, Paul and I soon learned what was nibbling at our bait—small silver trout. "Bait stealers," Paul said. They were too small to keep, and they depleted several of our shrimp. I looked around at other anglers and none of them seemed to be catching any noteworthy fish either. "Maybe we should head over to the lighthouse," I suggested.

"Just give it a little longer," Paul said. Patience and perhaps a good intuitive sense were some of Paul's other virtues.

I'm not sure if it was the bald eagle flying in from the coast, swooping low, or the osprey that soon followed, or the rising tide—maybe all three—but they seemed to signal the beginning of some real fishing. Speckled trout, almost all of them of legal size, soon began hitting our shrimp with intensity. Over the next hour, we began filling our cooler, Paul catching most of the fish, or course. Paul told me that my leader was too big and ugly; it was scaring the fish. He gave me one of his homemade rigs. After tying it onto my line, my luck started to improve.

When the fishing action paused, we pulled over to shore for a bathroom break. It was a small rocky beach almost hidden by marsh grass. Setting foot on the bank, stretching, we looked down and were amazed at how the ground was littered with pottery pieces and chipped chert (a soft flint-like stone). Native people, too, once came here to fish, people who used dugout canoes, while we were using one made of fiberglass. I picked up some of the orange, white and gray chert pieces and held them in my hands for a moment before returning them to the shoreline.

Man has always fished, I believe, as soon as he had the ability to do so. Predator and prey have an age-old bond, and if fishing with the right attitude and outdoor ethics, we fit in as much as the eagle and osprey. The tides pulse and so do the fish, it seems, back and forth with the flow—fish following fish, and man searching for his dinner.

Paul and I decided to make some casts from shore. It felt good to be able to move around. With a fully loaded canoe and two people, you just don't try to stand up.

As if by design, larger fish began to bite. Redfish! After a mighty struggle, Paul was able to reel his first one to within a few feet of shore, a whopper about three feet long. It shook itself loose just before I could bring the net under it. It was clearly over the legal size of 27 inches, but still a fun fight. We didn't stop there, and neither did the reds. I caught one about 23 inches and Paul caught a 22-inch one, both keepers.

Our struggles and shrieks of excitement drew some attention. Other anglers in fancy boats began forming a semi-circle around us. I wondered what they thought about two guys in an old canoe on shore, and one who had a pole repaired with silver duct tape (Paul's), but you can't argue with success. They gave us just enough room to cast.

The other anglers had puzzled looks on their faces when we got some more big hits and they didn't. One broke my line, so I quickly switched to my back-up pole. We caught a couple more reds and released them. I was pleased that some of Paul's luck was rubbing off on me. The other anglers just stared in wonder. It was almost funny, but I dared not laugh. I had seen the same scene play out time and again when fishing with Lucky Paul, like the gawkers who gather around the lucky winner at the roulette wheel, the guy the casino hates to see come through the door.

It was difficult to leave with the fishing so good, but we had a full cooler—our legal limit. We had to leave fish for the eagles, ospreys, dolphins and other anglers. This batch would feed our families for a month. I would view each meal of the Aucilla fish as a type of communion with a pristine place that had no factories, towns or subdivisions along its banks. Each bite would bring me closer to the water and marsh, the pulsing tides, the gnarled cypress and cedar, the river birds. Fish like that can't be anything but good for you.

I knew that when my last bag of fish in the freezer was consumed, it would be time to give Lucky Paul another call.

Canoe and Kayak Fishing Advantages

--Accessibility: You can reach those shallow and hard to reach areas and there are few worries about oyster bars, sand bars or getting trapped by low tide.
--Security: You're not dependent upon a motor and the myriad of things that can go wrong with it.
--Exercise: Paddling is great for your arms, shoulders and cardiovascular system.
--Cost effective: After a limited investment, it's just you and the paddle. And as far as public access, a sand launch area is generally preferred over an expensive concrete boat ramp.

Disadvantages

--Risk: Canoes and kayaks are generally not as stable as most other boats in windy, choppy conditions.
--Speed: You can't get to your favorite fishing areas as quickly.
--Distance: You don't want to take a canoe or kayak more than a couple of miles into the open Gulf or ocean.
--Space: You don't have as much room for gear, fish, and for personal space.

If You Go
The lower Aucilla River is located along U.S. 98 about twenty miles west of Perry and thirty miles southeast of Tallahassee. There are plenty of restaurants and places for lodging in both towns and there is a small bait store near the turn-off to the landing. The lower river has two landings that are clearly marked. One is just north of U.S. 98 about a half mile above the highway bridge on

the east side. The other is along a well graded road about three miles south of the bridge. The turn-off can be found about a mile and a half east of the bridge along Highway 98. Signs point the way.

Paul Force with a large cobia he caught in 2009.

18
Forgotten Coast Headwind

"They tell us that the natives of the region disappeared in the late sixteenth or early seventeenth century, at the time that white men began to penetrate Florida in numbers. There is no overlapping of white and Indian cultures in the top midden layers, no scraps of metal or imported European tools or ornaments, such as occur in diggings farther to the north, in the mission centers. The natives of this sea coast vanished abruptly from the land where their forebears had lived for thousands of years."
--Betty M. Watts, *The Watery Wilderness of Apalach, Florida*, 1975

Paddling into a headwind is not a good way to begin a three day sea kayaking trip. I was with my friend Dean and we were striking out from Indian Pass, a few miles southwest of the town of Apalachicola, heading east along Florida's Forgotten Coast. On our right was the 12,490-acre St. Vincent Island National Wildlife Refuge. To our left were the churning waters of Apalachicola Bay. Only after we embarked did I wonder why we didn't reverse the trip and paddle east to west *with* the prevailing wind?

We made slow progress, frequently stopping to rest along sandy shores littered with Indian pottery shards. Native people had lived, fished and hunted on this island for millennia, dating back to 240 A.D. They paddled the bay's waters in canoes they had chiseled out of old-growth pine or cypress trees. How did those crafts handle strong headwinds?

Native American names for this large triangular shaped land mass of 12,490 acres are not known. The current name was given by Franciscan friars in 1633 while visiting Apalachee Indians in the area. After the Apalachee Indians were dispersed, killed or captured by the English and their Creek allies in 1704, Creek and Seminoles Indians hunted and occasionally occupied the island throughout the latter half of the 1700s and early 1800s. They lost the island in 1811 as part of the Forbes Grant, a land for debt exchange in which the Indians forcibly gave up millions of acres of North Florida. Unlimited credit was alive even then until Indian hunters fell hopelessly behind despite traveling weeks at a time away from their families in search of deer skins, their primary trade commodity.

One of the earliest American owners of the island was George Hatch, who purchased the island at auction for $3,000 and used it for a private hunting and fishing preserve. His 1875 headstone near West Pass is the only marked grave on the island.

Perhaps the most colorful owner was Dr. Ray Pierce, a patent medicine king and developer of the Pierce-Arrow car, who bought the island in 1908. Pierce and his family used the island as a winter resort whereupon they feasted on venison, ducks, fish, oysters and sea turtle eggs most any day. "I counted 127 deer on one mile stretch of beach," read the journal of Charles Marks, whose father was a caretaker of the island for Dr. Pierce. "On the Gulf beach, it was easy on moonlight nights in the summer to find ten or fifteen turtle crawls in an evening, each containing 150 to 300 eggs. Mostly 'yellows', the eggs were best served scrambled, and were excellent in cakes." Marks said the turtles were large enough for a man to ride on their backs.

Pierce, not satisfied with the abundant native wildlife on the island, began to import non-native species—zebras, elands, German boars, Japanese deer, ring-necked pheasants, and the sambar deer from Asia. Most of the exotics eventually died out or were removed, unable to adapt. Only the elk-sized sambar deer remain.

The Nature Conservancy purchased the island in 1968 for $2.2 million and later sold it to the United States Fish and Wildlife Service for establishment as a wildlife refuge. Primitive weapons hunts of native deer, hogs and the sambar deer occur in fall and winter. The endangered red wolf was reintroduced in 1990 whereupon wolf families freely roam the uninhabited island. When the pups are weaned, they are taken to the Alligator River Refuge in North Carolina and are released. St. Vincent Island boasts the only wild wolf population in Florida.

Sambar deer track in the sand.

We rounded the southeast tip of St. Vincent Island and had a brief respite from the wind on the leeward side of a sand spit. There, on the beach, were the fresh tracks of the largest deer we had ever seen. Sambar! We scanned the shoreline and thick sabal palm forests, but didn't see any of the huge deer. We weren't disappointed, however. Arching sabal palms, many of which were falling into the bay from erosion, lined the shoreline for more than three miles to West Pass and the Gulf of Mexico. It was as tropical a scene as you'll find anywhere. "I can't believe we're in the United States," Dean exclaimed. "It's like Costa Rica!"

Even the nearby boats seemed like watercraft from another country or another time. They were the rugged wooden boats of oyster tongers who were working equally hard on this blustery day, if not more so, manning heavy wood tongs and pulling up the rock-like oyster clusters from the bay bottom. This method of oyster harvesting hasn't changed for generations. Seeing the tongers gave me a sudden appreciation for the biological richness of Apalachicola Bay--one of the most productive estuaries in North America--and the need to keep it viable.

I once joined a group of high school students in putting out various seine and plankton nets into the bay and was amazed to discover that every ounce of water teemed with life. We found numerous species of fish and thousands of tiny shrimp and zooplankton. This place where fresh and salt water joined together suddenly felt like a living organism.

After a brief lunch, we embarked on a straight five-mile shot across a corner of Apalachicola Bay to our destination on Cape St. George. More wind and waves. Dean and I drifted apart by a hundred feet or more and I was alone with my thoughts and the bay. At first I was nervous—bobbing up and down like a cork as occasional waves lapped over my bow and spray skirt. Gradually, however, I became more confident in my craft and my paddling skills, and thankful that my sea kayak had a rudder to help keep me heading in a straight path as I followed a reading on my GPS unit. I paddled the next hour and a half with some sense of reassurance for my safety.

Before the trip, I had come across another account of a trip across the bay, this one in a rowboat in 1879. It was part of a 2,600-mile journey down the Ohio and Mississippi Rivers and along the Gulf. "Following the coast on our left, numerous reefs of large and very fat oysters continually obstructed our progress," wrote Nathaniel H. Bishop. "We gathered a bushel with our hands in a very few minutes; but as the wind commenced to blow most spitefully, and the heavy forests of palms on the low shore offered a pleasant shelter, we disembarked about sunset in a magnificent grove of palmetto-trees, spending a pleasant evening in feasting upon the delicious bivalves, roasted and upon the half shell."

My arms felt like water-soaked logs when we landed on the uninhabited Cape St. George. We had been given permission to stay in the island's only structure, a government-owned cabin known as the Marshall House. We had the option of pitching our tents at a designated campsite a half mile away, but we gladly took the cabin. It was a storm-battered cypress-sided structure with a tin roof, an Old Florida relic nestled between coastal live oaks and slash pines. Solar panels had been added to generate just enough electricity for lights and a water pump. Inside, bleached bones, rusted tools and shells— relics from the bay and island—decorated shelves and the fireplace mantle. Tongue-and-groove pine walls and ceiling added to its rustic appearance. Most of the cabin's guests were biologists studying the bay or barrier island environment.

After settling in, we explored the bay shoreline. Many of the pines had been cat-faced to extract sap for turpentine in the 1930s and 40s, pines that were now being washed into the bay. Barrier islands are always shifting, and sea level rise is causing them to shrink in size. There is no better example of that fact than the Cape St. George Lighthouse. First erected in 1833, it was moved two miles to the east in 1847 before being flattened by a powerful gale in 1851. The lighthouse was then moved inland more than four hundred yards from the Gulf. Here it remained through civil war and hurricanes until coastal erosion gradually stripped away the beach and waves began to relentlessly pound the lighthouse base, tilting the structure and then toppling it in 2005. The lighthouse lay in pieces in the surf, but through painstaking efforts, it was reconstructed on nearby St. George Island and is now a major attraction. "We tried to look at the bright side of it, and said 'Well, if you can dig a dinosaur up out of the ground and put the bones back together in a museum, we can dig this lighthouse up and put the pieces back together,'" Dennis Barnell, president of the St. George Lighthouse Association, told *USA Today*. "It's somewhat of a miracle."

To explore the island further, Dean and I hiked to the ocean side of the island down a sugar-sand road through hordes of salt marsh mosquitoes. We couldn't walk fast enough. The bugs retreated only when we reached the Gulf shoreline with its strong breeze and pounding surf. We relished a white sand beach with no human footprints, mostly driftwood and crab tracks. "This has to be one of the most uninhabited stretches of beach left in Florida," Dean said. Nearing sunset, we raced back to the cabin through the mosquito gauntlet and cooked a delicious freeze-dried dinner on a real stove.

We slept soundly that night, the sleep of two people who had paddled fifteen miles into a headwind.

Just after sunrise, Dean paddled into the bay with fishing pole at the ready. Casting a plastic jig, he soon caught two speckled trout. We rummaged through the cupboards, found corn meal, oil and seasoning, and fried up our breakfast. As we munched on the delicate white meat, two white-haired guests arrived by boat. They introduced themselves as Joe Barber and Eleanor Hillman, brother and sister. Their family had a long history with the island, they said, beginning with their grandfather,

Edward G. Porter, who was the keeper of the island's lighthouse from the late 1800s until his untimely death in 1913. He owned the island at the time. The island once had a schoolhouse and several cottages before being taken over by the military in the 1940's so soldiers could practice beach assaults.

While the state paid $8.5 million for the nine-mile long Cape St. George in 1977, Joe remembered when "you couldn't give away these islands because of taxes."

Joe worked as a commercial fisherman and guide for most of his life. "We'd go out for three or four days at a time," he said. "We hardly ever came back with under 1,500 pounds with three men working. One time, three of us in a little 36-foot boat caught 4,270 pounds of snapper in less than twenty-four hours." They returned to the site and caught another 3,900 pounds of mixed grouper and snapper. "I've made a living on eight different boats," he concluded.

"And I can't believe you came all the way over here in those little boats," said Eleanor with a chuckle, nodding to our kayaks.

Later, I learned that Joe's boat skills came in handy when he aided in the rescue of survivors of the English tanker *Mica* that had been torpedoed by a German U-boat in 1942 about twenty miles off Cape San Blas. He and a friend towed in another rescue boat that had run out of gas in Apalachicola Bay. "Actually, I helped pull the survivors in," he said in *Voices of the Apalachicola* by Faith Eidse. "Some of them were hurt, some of 'em just had their underclothes on, they had to abandon the ship so quick. Some of 'em had jumped down in their lifeboats and hurt their legs and ankles." Nineteen sailors died in the attack. The *Mica* has since become a reef that attracts numerous fish and other sea life and is considered a living memorial.

Joe ended his career on the water as a boat captain for the Florida State University Marine Laboratory at St. Theresa a few miles from Carrabelle.

The synchronicity of meeting two people with a history for the island and the cabin was not lost upon Dean and I. We allowed our new friends to roam through the cabin while we loaded our kayaks. Once paddling east again to the sound of calling eagles, we were greeted by our old friend, the headwind. It was stronger than ever, but having already experienced some of the magic of a paddling journey, we simply bore through it with a renewed sense of innocence and hope for what lay ahead.

Eleanor Hillman and Joe Barber have had a
long relationship with Cape St. George.

If You Go

The Forgotten Coast is marked by unspoiled barrier islands and peninsulas, and small coastal villages such as Apalachicola, Eastpoint and Carrabelle. It is part of segments four and five of the Florida Circumnavigational Saltwater Paddling Trail, a 1,515-mile sea kayaking trail around Florida's entire coast (see "The Wild Wind of Apalachee Bay"). While no camping is allowed on St. Vincent Island, there are several trail campsites on both Cape St. George and St. George Island. Most were established by the Apalachicola National Estuarine Research Reserve.

As far as winds are concerned, a north wind would be the worst case scenario for paddling inside the barrier islands since the fetch—the length of water over which a given wind has blown—can be several miles long. This means that the waves would be hitting one's boat broadside. A headwind is generally easier to navigate in terms of kayak stability than a broadside wind. A south wind wouldn't be too bothersome (except for crossing open passes) since the islands provide a barrier, and a tailwind is generally helpful.

Since Apalachicola Bay is open water, a sea kayak with a rudder and sprayskirt is recommended. Calm weather is fine for beginners, but this stretch is generally recommended for paddlers who are have knowledge of basic paddling strokes and who have experience in open water conditions. Plus, current in the passes can be strong during peak tidal changes and may require a wide sweep around them.

The string of barrier islands—St. Vincent, Cape St. George and St. George—can be accessed from either end. The closest public boat ramp to St. Vincent Island is located 22 miles west of Apalachicola at the end of County Road 30-B at Indian Pass. It is one quarter mile across the pass to the island. The island is not accessible by land. Kayak rentals are available a few miles away along St. Joe Bay at Happy Ours Kayak, 850-229-1991.

For St. George Island, the access is on the east side of the main bridge (off of Highway 98 at Eastpoint) where the bridge meets the island. Public access is available in St. George Island State Park as well on the east end of the island. Kayak rentals are available on the island at Journeys of St. George Island, 850-927-3259.

Dog Island, the easternmost island in the Forgotten Coast barrier island chain, is privately owned and no camping is allowed, although kayakers can visit on day trips.

The tropical looking St. Vincent Point.

20
The Wild Wind of Apalachee Bay

The great sea has set me in motion
Set me adrift,
And I move as a weed in the river.

The arch of sky
And mightiness of storms
Encompasses me,
And I am left
Trembling with joy
--Eskimo Song

Wind over water always seems colder, especially
when it's a bone-chilling northeast wind gusting at
fifteen to twenty miles per hour. Forget the fact that Matt
Keene and I were paddling in the "Sunshine State"—

winter refuge for millions of people from northern climates. This was North Florida in late December and 38 degrees was 38 degrees! I yearned for a ski mask to temper biting cold that stung my face.

We felt somewhat foolish as we aimed down the Aucilla River along Florida's Big Bend Coast. Both Matt and I knew that paddling on this day was slightly insane, and neither of us would have gone out alone, but Matt was completing a first-ever thru-paddle on the entire 1,515-mile Florida Circumnavigational Saltwater Paddling Trail. Since I had mapped the coastal trail for three years for the state's Office of Greenways and Trails, linking together existing trails wherever possible such as the FWC's Big Bend Saltwater Paddling Trail, I had taken a keen interest in Matt's progress. I felt privileged to join him for three days.

Matt had embarked more than three months earlier from Ft. Clinch State Park above Jacksonville. He headed south along the Intracoastal Waterway, rounded the Keys and Ten Thousand Islands, and paddled north along the Gulf Coast. He had braved heat, cold, bugs and storms and had *only* 250 miles to go before reaching the finish line at Big Lagoon State Park near the Alabama border. A reception was planned less than two weeks hence, so Matt didn't want too many delays. He had already waited out a storm the previous day as a guest at my house and he was going to spend Christmas at his parents' home in Clermont. Windy cold weather was just par for the course.

Dolphins drew our attention. They were chasing mullet with abandon, thrashing the water and sending silvery fish through the air. Cold snaps often drive mullet, trout and redfish up the warmer coastal rivers and the dolphins were following them.

A young bald eagle called from a cypress snag, marking the end of the trees. Before us, only vast expanses of needlerush and cordgrass were visible along the shores. Where the grass ended, windswept water and oyster bars lay ahead—the Gulf of Mexico. We paddled out to deeper water, still pushed by the wind, then we turned west into Apalachee Bay. The full force of the north wind hit us at an angle from the rear, almost at a broadside. Waves slapped over our bows. I cinched up my spray skirt.

Matt had experienced plenty of challenging weather on his journey. During the long open water crossing of Florida Bay from the Keys, in which he was accompanied by friend Matt Gallagher, the wind and waves picked up on the third day. "We experienced a washing machine of two to four foot swells that were chaotic," he said. "It was hard to paddle in with knowing that you had no options to rest or get out of it. You just had to paddle through it until you reached the coastline of Cape Sable. That was intimidating and strengthening at the same time. The opportunity for storms to develop is something that has presented a challenge almost every single afternoon, especially in the warmer periods."

Along Apalachee Bay, it wasn't a washing machine effect—more like a steady stream of rolling waves. And because the wind was keeping the tide out, we had to stay well off shore, so there was no option to land for nearly eight miles. In other words, no opportunity for a bathroom break. The cold weather and my morning tea had prompted an urgent call of nature. "Hey Matt," I called out, "how do you use the bathroom in these conditions?"

Matt smiled knowingly, chugged a vitamin soda, and tossed me the empty bottle. "Use this," he said, "but you have to get the angle just right." I wasn't entirely successful given the rocking ocean, kind of like trying to pee on a bucking bronco, but it relieved the discomfort.

Matt had paddled most of the trail with Matt Gallagher and girlfriend Jodi Eller, but both had dropped out at different points along the Gulf. During Jodi's last stint with Matt near Yankeetown at the southern end of Florida's Big Bend, the couple was turned away from the Gulf by bad weather. They set up camp beneath a pavilion at the western end of the Cross Florida Greenway, a paved multi-use trail along the now defunct Cross Florida Barge Canal. Even this shelter was not enough. The slanting rain was driving so hard they retreated to a spot beneath the pavilion floor with a tarp over them, huddling and shivering. "We were soaked to the bone, chilled, and worst of all, covered in sand," Matt recalled. "There is absolutely nothing worse than wet, sandy clothes. Nothing." Fortunately, Matt and Jodi were rescued by a kind trail maintenance worker who drove them to a motel.

With our situation in Apalachee Bay, the sun shone and we were not stranded. We were still able to paddle, though in less than ideal conditions. If we tipped, we could have stood up in waist deep frigid water. The only problem—no other boats bobbed along the horizon. If the wind became too much and we had to slog to shore and walk out, we'd be lucky to make it to a paved road by nightfall. It's the only drawback of paddling along a remote and carefully protected shoreline—part of the St. Marks National Wildlife Refuge—one that appears as wild and pristine as when the first Spaniards landed in the 1500s.

The wind slowed as we neared Palmetto Island, a crescent spit of land shaded by sabal palms. Upon landing,

I examined a large flake of worked chert left by early native people. Amazingly, it was still sharp after all of these hundreds or even thousands of years. I left it where I found it. Shrubs of St. Johns wort and yaupon blocked most of the wind as we munched on tuna fish and crackers.

Sitting there with Matt, with his weathered skin, long red beard and hair, and worn clothes, he looked like someone who had paddled this coast for several weeks. He was only twenty-three years old, but he seemed older. His maturity had showed in the care he had taken in preparing for the journey. After earning and saving money by scraping barnacles off boats, he had crafted his own wood kayak from a kit and carved a West Greenland style paddle from a cedar two-by-four. He and Jodi had prepared food for the journey with a solar food dryer they had made. He sewed together his own sleeping bag. "Long distance journeys have different considerations than weekend or day trips," Matt said. "You have to really examine everything you are carrying and decide if it is essential or not. As you progress in your journey, your needs become simplified, and with that comes a simpler view of living your life. You shed the weight of civilization—the stress, the doubt, the body fat… Your confidence rises and you learn to live day by day."

Regarding his last few days of solo paddling, he said, "It allowed a lot of time for introspection. I've seen the coast with a different set of eyes, with a new outlook. I wouldn't necessarily recommend taking such a long trip by yourself; you miss out on what you can gain with friends, as well as the safety issues. But I do think that time by yourself is necessary and healthy."

Matt reminded me of stories I had heard about people who once led a nomadic-type existence along Florida's remote Big Bend Coast. One old timer called them "the island people" because they often stayed on coastal tree islands in the region. They mostly fished and traded for what they needed, leading a simple life. Many are believed to have had Muscogee Creek/Seminole Indian heritage.

Maybe Matt epitomized the spirit of the drifters. He was the first of what could become a steady stream of sea kayakers who would follow the country's longest coastal paddling trail, experiencing adventure, challenge, beauty and acts of kindness. Living a simple life.

Ending the first day at the St. Marks Lighthouse.

From Palmetto Island, a strong tailwind helped us to easily cruise toward the St. Marks Lighthouse, four miles away, where my wife Cyndi would pick us up for the night. The weather had warmed by ten degrees and we leisurely paddled and talked. The challenges of the morning were behind us; we simply cherished what the coast and trail had to offer.

By the time we launched again the next morning, the temperature was hovering around 40 degrees. Cold wind was gusting like the day before, only this time more from the east. Once Matt and I pushed off from the lighthouse and hit the mouth of the St. Marks River, the wind's full force hit us. Fortunately, it was a tailwind. For nearly seven miles, we surfed to Shell Point on three-foot whitecaps. Once I got over my initial nervousness, it was fun. Ducks and other birds didn't seem to mind, either. Flocks of buffleheads, scaup and redheads bobbed up and down on the surface, along with several long-necked loons. Apalachee Bay was a bird haven in winter.

The fortuitous tailwind, moving us along at a faster pace than expected, also eliminated the need for the "call of nature" bottle. The extra benefits were much appreciated.

At a coastal park in Shell Point, we were met by a volunteer with the Florida Paddling Trails Association, Garry Breedlove of Tallahassee. Association members serve as volunteer stewards of the circumnavigational trail and other Florida paddling trails. Garry was kind enough to serve an exquisite lunch of roast chicken, cranberry sauce, chips and hot chocolate. It was in appreciation of Matt, who was serving as a noteworthy trail ambassador on his thru paddle.

The wind had calmed when Matt and I started paddling another seven mile stretch of open water to a peninsula at the end of the Ochlockonee River known as

Mashes Sands. It was easy to talk and Matt even made a cell phone call. Suddenly, from the south, four foot swells emerged and Matt and I experienced a roller coaster ride of waves. When Matt dipped down into a trough, I could only see his upper body, his kayak obscured by water. "It always amazes me how quickly conditions can change," he said upon landing at Mashes Sands.

"And if we were facing a strong headwind," I said, "that would have slowed us considerably. I'm not sure we would reach our destination by dark."

By the end of the day, as we crossed the wide Ochlockonee River and paddled up Chaires Creek in Bald Point State Park to a primitive campsite, it was dead calm. No-see-ums stirred. A bald eagle called from a dead pine. White egrets flew up from a nearby marsh and disappeared into the grass again. After nearly eighteen miles of paddling, we soon landed and set up camp in a tree-covered peninsula that overlooked a wilderness of marsh, water and pines. As the sun faded and Venus emerged brightly shining, I reflected on the contrasts we had seen during the day and evening. To paddle part of the circumnavigational trail was to develop an appreciation of the sea's power and unpredictability, and also to cherish calm moments when Florida's coastal beauty was on full display. And it helps to have a tailwind.

Matt Keene completed his historic journey on January 5th, 2009, at Big Lagoon State Park near Pensacola. A group of friends, family, media and local government officials greeted him. "It was very humbling," he concluded. "It really let me experience everything Florida has to offer."

Matt Keene signs trail logbook at Big Lagoon State Park near Pensacola, ending a 1,515-mile journey.

More about the Florida Circumnavigational Saltwater Paddling Trail

Kayak enthusiast David Gluckman conceived the idea of the circumnavigational trail, or CT, in the mid-1980s. He was inspired by the success of the 350-mile Maine Islands Trail network. In 2004, the state of Florida pursued Gluckman's dream, based in part on the successful completion of the 105-mile Big Bend Saltwater Paddling Trail from the Aucilla River to the town of Suwannee. The Florida Department of Environmental Protection's Office of Greenways and Trails began scouting and mapping the trail, and by the end of 2007, most of the CT was complete.

In all, CT travelers have access to more than 80 primitive campsites, including some on remote islands. Motels and public and private campgrounds are available for other overnight stops and countless coastal parks provide rest stops. An important purpose of the trail is to expose paddlers to Florida's rich history and fragile coastal environment. Points of interest include lighthouses, Indian temple mounds, and museums. Access points for the trail number in the hundreds, and restaurants and re-supply opportunities abound as well.

Every type of Florida coastal habitat type can be encountered along the trail, from barrier island dune systems to salt marshes to mangroves. Paddlers may see manatees, dolphins, American crocodiles, alligators, sea turtles, a host of fish, rays and crabs, and birds ranging from bald eagles to brightly-colored warblers. The CT traverses a splendid array of protected lands, including 18 national wildlife refuges, 37 aquatic preserves, 47 Florida state parks, two national parks, two national seashores, a national marine sanctuary, and numerous local parks and preserves. The summer of 2007 marked a major milestone for the trail when the United States Department of Interior designated it a national recreation trail.

Local support for the trail is growing. The City of Miami and Dade County helped to organize a dedication of the Biscayne portion of the trail in 2007, and John Pennekamp State Park organized a similar dedication for the Keys segment the year before. Such recognition will help ensure the trail's success, which largely depends upon partnerships with outfitters, paddling clubs and various government entities.

In many regions, especially in southwest Florida, the trail connects to county "blueways" trail networks geared towards paddlers. More local governments are establishing new paddling trails and campsites. The CT's continued success will also be ensured by the support of

the newly formed Florida Paddling Trails Association. ⸜
This nonprofit organization will help maintain and
improve the CT and other paddling trails. Members can
access information about the CT and more than 150
shorter paddling trails on the association's Web site.

The trail begins at Big Lagoon State Park near
Pensacola, only a few paddle strokes from the Alabama
border. The route follows an inside passage along several
barrier islands and skirts between two historic Civil War
era forts and other points of interest. At Destin, the trail
breaks out into the Gulf of Mexico along the quartz-sand
beaches of the Emerald Coast. Unspoiled stretches of
public land are interspersed between motels, restaurants
and resort communities. The "new urbanist" master-
planned community of Seaside, where parts of the movie
The Truman Show featuring Jim Carey was filmed, is
adjacent to Grayton Beach State Park, an overnight stop
on the trail.

Panama City's St. Andrews State Park marks the
beginning of a 400-mile stretch that can best be described
as "Old Florida." It includes unspoiled coastal peninsulas,
wild barrier islands, dynamic bays and estuaries, and
unmarred vistas of salt marsh, tree islands and winding
tidal creeks. Few signs of humans can be found along vast
stretches of public land such as the St. Marks National
Wildlife Refuge, the Big Bend Wildlife Management
Area, the Lower Suwannee National Wildlife Refuge and
the Waccasassa Bay Preserve State Park.

Along the Crooked River through Tate's Hell
Swamp State Forest, paddlers have a high likelihood of
spotting a Florida black bear, a protected species. Small
coastal towns in this region, some of which are historic
fishing communities, add a cultural flavor. Manatees are

commonly seen around Crystal River and Homosassa Springs.

Pinellas County just above Tampa Bay marks the beginning of the more populous southwest Florida coast, but paddlers can still explore undeveloped islands and peninsulas, along with historic sites and points of interest. The trail links to several county "blueways." These are extensive networks of marked paddling trails through bays, rivers, tidal creeks and along barrier islands. Then the trail dips into the remote Ten Thousand Islands, a maze of undeveloped mangrove islands and tidal creeks that once served as a refuge for recluses and outlaws; the area is now a haven for wilderness lovers. At Everglades City, paddlers can choose either a sheltered route of backwater streams known as the Wilderness Waterway, or a coastal island route for several days of uninterrupted paddling through Everglades National Park.

The Florida Keys offers tropical splendor and a unique maritime culture. Paddlers can wind through lush mangrove tunnels, peer into gin clear waters rich with marine life, and also dock at locally-owned restaurants and bars that often feature musical entertainment. History comes alive, too, as the trail includes visual reminders of Henry Flagler's overseas railroad of the early 1900s. Kayakers can paddle alongside arching concrete columns of the original Seven Mile Bridge between Knight's Key and Ohio Key as well as other historic railroad bridges that survived the infamous Labor Day Hurricane of 1935. Points of interest include Indian Key Historic State Park, the site of a Seminole raid on an early homestead in the 1830s. And just southwest of the park is the San Pedro Underwater Archeological Preserve. In good weather, paddlers can glide over or snorkel the remains of a 1733

Spanish treasure ship, which lies in eighteen feet of water. The reefs and waters of the Keys were once treacherous to shipping. For decades, salvaging shipwrecks, known as wrecking, was the main livelihood of the local population.

Heading north from the Keys, the trail traverses North America's largest marine park in the United States National Park System, Biscayne National Park, featuring shallow patch reefs and tropical fish. A mask and snorkel are suggested items to bring. From Oleta River State Park in northern Biscayne Bay, paddlers have the option of taking either the Intracoastal Waterway or the Atlantic shore, depending upon weather conditions. While motel stays are necessary for some nights, the region features lighthouses, museums, palm-lined beaches and balmy winter weather. Near Jupiter, paddlers can explore the unspoiled Loxahatchee River, Florida's first national wild and scenic river, and camp at Jonathan Dickinson State Park.

Paddling the Indian River Lagoon.

Manatees and bird rookeries abound in sections of the trail through the Indian River Lagoon, Banana Lagoon, the Merritt Island National Wildlife Refuge and Mosquito Lagoon. Camping opportunities are numerous on the many tree-covered man-made and natural islands along the Intracoastal Waterway. One popular activity near Cape Canaveral is to view a space shuttle lift-off from a kayak.

For a cultural break, paddlers can stay in St. Augustine's historic district and stroll through North America's oldest European-founded city, or they can participate in one of the city's nightly ghost tours. The tours give new meaning to the term "living history."

The last stretch of the trail boasts unspoiled stretches of public lands, mazes of tidal creeks, coastal bluffs, numerous sea islands and historic plantations. The trail's terminus is at Fort Clinch, a Civil War era fort along the Georgia border and now part of a state park.

Whatever your paddling interest, the 1,515-mile circumnavigational trail serves up rich and rewarding experiences and unsurpassed coastal beauty.

If You Go

Paddling all or part of the Florida Circumnavigational Saltwater Paddling Trail can be the experience of a lifetime. What better way to see and experience a wide diversity of coastal environments and marine life? However, users should first become aware of the trail's realities.

Paddlers on the trail can encounter strong winds and currents, open water stretches, busy boat channels and various types of weather. In several stretches, one must paddle more than twenty miles to reach a legal campsite or motel. For this reason, proper experience, conditioning and equipment, and awareness of weather forecasts and wind conditions, are all imperative. Paddlers should be skilled at using a GPS system since the trail is marked by GPS points on a map, not by signs. Cell phone coverage can be spotty in some sections.

Generally, it is best to avoid the summer hurricane season for a long distance journey. Recommended paddling months are late October through April. Bugs and hot steamy weather, along with lightning storms, will be less prevalent.

Allowing for some days off, paddlers should plan on taking about four months to traverse the entire trail. While every effort has been made to provide low cost or free campsites for paddlers, motel stays will occasionally be necessary. Waterfront motels, and some established campgrounds, can be expensive, depending on the season and locale, so long-distance paddlers should budget accordingly. Many motels and campgrounds, especially in south Florida and the Keys during peak seasons (holidays and early spring), require advance reservations in order to be assured a spot.

Long-distance paddlers should plan on having four to seven days worth of supplies at any given time, depending on the segment (the trail is divided into 26 segments). The longest stretch without an opportunity to re-supply will be from Everglades City to Flamingo in segment 14, covering about a hundred miles. In some trail towns, care packages can be sent ahead to post offices in care of general delivery.

Paddlers will be able to replenish water supplies almost daily in developed sections of the trail due to the many parks along the route. However, in the Big Bend and Ten Thousand Islands in particular, fresh water re-supply opportunities can be spaced several days apart. The general rule is to figure on one gallon of water per person per day. Users should be mindful that animals such as raccoons on remote coastal islands may seek out fresh water as much as food. Paddlers should hang food and water or store in secure hatches.

Interested paddlers should peruse all segment guides, maps and associated Web sites beforehand to aid in planning, and be sure to leave a detailed float plan with a reliable friend or relative before beginning a journey.

Besides long distance paddles, every segment of the CT can be utilized for day trips and weekend excursions. Paddlers may also want to opt to do the entire trail in sections over several years, similar to how many thru-hikers backpack the Appalachian Trail.

To learn more about the Florida Circumnavigational Saltwater Paddling Trail, and to download free maps and trails guides, log onto www.floridagreenwaysandtrails.com. For information about the Florida Paddling Trails Association, log onto www.floridapaddlingtrails.com/.

21
Vicarious Paddling

"Vicarious: Felt or undergone as if one were taking part in the experience or feelings of another."
--*American Heritage Dictionary*

With the advent of Internet blogs and a handy device known as the SPOT Messenger—a type of GPS tracking system that can instantaneously send a paddler's position to a website and e-mail address—it is now possible to follow along with paddlers on long-distance journeys. This can be both good and bad. Good in that you can see that friends and relatives are safe and can vicariously join with them, but bad in that you might want to physically join but can't for various reasons. You might be trying to make ends meet, stuck in an office or some other indoor job, while those carefree paddlers are out enjoying blue waters under blue skies.

Here's an entry from paddler Dan Dick who joined his friend Mike Ruso on a thru-paddle on the entire Florida Circumnavigational Saltwater Paddling Trail in 2008 and early 2009: "We have seen dolphins a plenty! They all seem to be going in the same direction as ourselves, leading to the conclusion that somewhere along our path there must be some great dolphin city where they teach themselves to do tricks and the seas are full of fish."

Doesn't that make you just want to paddle in open water with a school of dolphins?

Matt Keene, described in the previous chapter, also kept a blog about paddling the entire circumnavigational trail in 2008 and early 2009. Here's how he described paddling along the tip of the Everglades and Florida Bay in early November:

> Pristine, shell lined beaches with swaying palm trees. Nine-and-a-half miles of uninterrupted white sand coastline, lacking even in footprints. Silence. Solitude. Big deer roaming the shore in the early dawn hours. Crocodiles patrolling the shallows in the sunset hours. Big, fat eastern diamondbacks residing in the shady hardwood hammocks of their kingly domain. Sharks drifting in and out with the waves as they search for their nightly meals. Dolphins slapping the surface of the water and leaping into the air as they play like adolescents with their prey.

We still have a lot of Florida to discover and explore. Every week brings a new change and special treasures. There may be new places that challenge for the title, but if the Everglades isn't the beating heart of the state, pumping with history and vitality, lightly touched by man, then it has certainly captured mine.

I wish I could tell you the events that took place in this marvelous place, the things we saw, but here is a glimpse. ... Just imagine a place in your mind where you find silence. A place where the world around you grows and grows. Where everything seems larger than life, and wild. A place where the wild Florida you imagine, actually lives and breathes.

God, doesn't that just inspire you to hop in your kayak and paddle to the wildest place you know?

But reality slips into these blogs, too. Take this entry from Dan and Mike after camping on the remote Cape St. George Preserve along Florida's Forgotten Coast and discovering sand gnats (no-see-ums) for the first time: "They're the most awful things on earth. They're tiny— they look like flecks of pepper, and because of their small size they could never bite something as large as ourselves. Luckily for them they don't have to. They spit acid onto you and then slurp up the dissolved flesh and blood. So not only is it itchy and maddening, it's also disgusting. We were so plagued by the things that we didn't eat dinner that night because we didn't want to leave our tents (in order to run the stoves). In the morning we made a mad dash to the kayaks and hit the water without breakfast. Not to make it seem like everything is terrible, but that day a front rolled in on us and brought with it rain and angry winds."

Bugs and nasty weather. What could be worse while kayak camping?

Mike described an age old seafaring mystery they encountered. "One afternoon Dan and I both heard what we thought was a girl calling out to us, but there was no one around," he wrote. "There was nothing for miles except the wind and the waves. Sirens and sea madness, I'm serious."

After reading about their adventures for several days, I couldn't sit still any longer. Through Dan and Mike's SPOT Messenger readings on their blog, I tracked their movements one morning and determined that they would be paddling from Ochlockonee Bay to Spring Creek that day, only fifteen miles from my house. So, in a steady drizzle, I loaded my sea kayak onto my car and headed towards the coast. After launching, I avoided the windy main channel and took a short-cut to the Gulf via a winding tidal creek, hoping to intercept Dan and Mike. The creek emptied into an obstacle course of exposed oyster bars. Once I completed the maze, I faced open water. The rain had stopped, but it was still gray, cold and lonely feeling. I repeatedly scanned the horizon. Various grassy islands, some with small tree clumps, could be seen, but no kayaks. Only some floating black and white bufflehead ducks.

I paddled and searched, paddled and searched. Nothing. Dan and Mike could be anywhere. Maybe they stayed another night along Ochlocknee Bay until the weather improved, or stopped short at one of the islands. My efforts weren't a total loss, however. The lure of meeting two thru-paddlers with whom I had exchanged e-mails had gotten me off my duff and into the wild and raw Big Bend Coast. I had often likened this section of the trail as four hundred miles of old coastal Florida—vast expanses of salt marsh, tree islands, tidal creeks and small villages. It was both humbling and inspiring to paddle just a piece of it.

Letting go of my expectations at finding two thru-paddlers, I rounded a point and made my way up the main channel back to Spring Creek. As I neared the ramp where I had first launched, I spotted two blue kayaks and two young men retrieving gear from their hatches. Dan and Mike! While I was taking the short-cut, they had followed the main channel and missed me. We warmly greeted each other and they gladly accepted my offer of dinner at the famous Spring Creek Restaurant a block away.

First, we toured the shoreline with Lee Spears, the eighty-year-old proprietor of the small RV park where Dan and Mike were staying. A sixth-generation commercial fisherman, Lee showed us the old tin-roofed house where he was raised and walked us through a white concrete block building that once housed his crab picking business. Spring Creek was a small traditional fishing village that had been slowly ebbing away since passage of a Florida ban on large mullet fishing nets in 1994, one that I featured in my book *Waters Less Traveled*.

That evening, over all-you-can-eat catfish, I sat and listened to Mike and Dan's tales of adventure. It was far better than reading a blog. Dan had been a novice kayaker at the start of the trip and didn't bring a spray skirt. On the second day, waves inundated his cockpit while they crossed the wind-blown mouth of Pensacola Bay. Luckily, he kept his kayak upright and emptied it with a bilge pump. The two had also camped out during several freezing nights and had endured consecutive days of rain, but the hospitable people they met kept their spirits high. Only 1,338 miles to go!

Before bidding them farewell, I gave Dan and Mike some proven sand gnat repellent and a list of "trail angels" they could call upon along the route. If I couldn't live my own long-distance adventure, it felt good to help someone else live theirs, even in small ways.

Over the next few days and weeks, I found myself fretting about Dan and Mike when the winds kicked up and storms threatened. A thousand things could go wrong; I just hoped they didn't. I felt a bit like a parent. Worrying about people on long-distance journeys hasn't changed much since early times, even with modern tracking technology. And so I kept checking their blog and said a prayer or two. And I dreamed of taking my own long-distance paddling journey on the CT.

On March 26, 2009, Mike and Dan safely completed their 1,515-mile journey at Ft. Clinch State Park above Jacksonville across from the Georgia border, making them the second and third thru paddlers of the trail.

More About Long-Distance Florida Paddlers

To learn about people who have paddled the entire Florida Circumnavigational Saltwater Paddling trail and who are currently paddling the trail, log onto the paddling community link of the Florida Paddling Trails Association website: http://www.floridapaddlingtrails.com. Blog links are often included. To learn about long distance races around Florida, check out the website for The Water Tribe: http://www.watertribe.com/.

*Dan Dick and Mike Ruso at journey's end, Fort
Clinch State Park along the Georgia border.*

The wide floodplain of the restored Kissimmee River.

22
Kissimmee River Dream

"As far as the eye can see at times, there is a vast sea of vivid green rolling onward toward the horizon. The banks are lined with small trees and shrubs, which in spring burst into flowers and new foliage, and it is a very paradise of gorgeous, if unmusical, birds that fill the air with their croaking and screaming."
--Nevin O. Winter, *Florida the Land of Enchantment*, 1918

With a few exceptions, most natural history writers rarely make much money on their books. For example, when I received my first royalty check in early 2010 for *New Dawn for the Kissimmee River*, an account of kayaking with a high profile expedition from Orlando to Lake Okeechobee down the Kissimmee chain of lakes and restored Kissimmee River, I determined that my wallet would have been fatter had I worked one evening a week at the local Chevron station during the many months I worked on the book. Still, there were other rewards, such as reading published reviews of the book.

Here's an unedited excerpt from a review on EBay from someone called Fishphart: "Alot of self congratulatory back-slapping by the tree huggers going on here. They make it obvious that they truly despise ANY kind of developement anywhere unless of course its by one of their own, such as Robert Redford building a ski resort / real estate developement right smack dap in a pristine range of mountains. The only thing lacking was a Big Brass Band floating down the river with them as they ate granola bars, trail mix and other 'sustainable' food sources."

Ouch. This guy has some real issues about tree huggers. I guess we were supposed to hunt and gather all of our own food on the journey, and distance ourselves from any real or imagined association with Robert Redford.

In all fairness to my ego, some readers—mostly friends—wrote complimentary reviews on Amazon and WorldCat. And tree-hugging groups such as Sierra Club Florida and the Florida Wildlife Federation promoted the book on websites and in their newsletters. Every bit helped since it can be tough getting positive attention for one book out of the millions published. And yes, I would have gratefully accepted assistance from Robert Redford had he offered.

Soon after that first paltry royalty check, Dan Cotter of the South Florida Water Management District called and asked if I could meet him at the Kissimmee River to begin identifying potential camps for a top-notch paddling trail through the Kissimmee valley. It was a follow-up to our 2007 expedition. Even though this exciting project fit in with my job as coordinator of paddling trails for the state, I hesitated. Travel money had been so drastically cut that I was often driving my own car and paying for my own travel expenses for state business, and the Kissimmee River was a long ways from Talla-hassee. Another hit to my wallet. But the Kissimmee has a pull that is difficult to resist, like a pilgrimage site that seems to call its followers. And so I traveled the 400 miles to the Riverwoods Field Lab on the Kissimmee River near Bassinger. There, I met with Dan and two of his associates along with paddlers Bill Redmon of Lake Wales and Frances Howell Coleman of Winter Haven.

Bill was past director of the Lake Aurora Christian Camp near Lake Wales. He had instigated a wilderness program at the camp that featured 25-foot canoes requiring several paddlers each in order to promote "team building." One motivation for his interest in the Kissimmee trail was to lead trips down the river. Also, he explained, "I like to see things come together."

Another of Bill's goals was to develop a compatible relationship with airboaters since airboating is an historic use in the area and paddling is not, at least not in the post-dugout canoe era. "I'm more worried about the attitude of paddlers toward airboaters than vice versa," he said.

For Frances, a widow of Kissimmee restoration champion Richard Coleman—who was killed in an airboat accident—her interest was to diversify use on the river by promoting more canoeing and kayaking. She had been urging Polk County officials to develop a county-wide blueways system, one that would include part of the Kissimmee Basin. Plus, her motives were personal. "Richard would have loved this project!" she said.

Soon after our introductions, Dan told me, "Your book is one of the drivers for this project. It's being waved around at our meetings as proof that the potential is there for paddlers to use the trail." Slowly, my original idealism for writing the book began to well up inside.

After poring over maps, we set out by vehicle to investigate potential spots along the river for future river camps. A river camp generally consists of a screened pavilion, picnic table, fire ring, and a chemical or composting toilet. It's a step up from basic primitive camping and it's helping to draw paddlers to other places that have them such as the Suwannee River, Okefenokee National Wildlife Refuge, and Everglades National Park. Several locations along the Kissimmee we viewed that day seemed suitable, and most were shaded by old-growth live oak and sabal palm trees.

One spot in a live oak hammock provided a broad view of a soon-to-be restored section of the Kissimmee. A vast cow pasture now covered the wide river floodplain. From talking with scientists, I knew that the pasture would quickly transform to freshwater marsh once periodic flooding was allowed again; long dormant seeds would come to life quicker than anyone could imagine. The scene here would be made all the more dramatic by a planned viewing tower. Paddlers would love it. No other

Florida river has a two to three mile wide marshy floodplain that gives one the feeling they are paddling through the lower Everglades' famous "River of Grass." In all, 43 miles of the original meandering Kissimmee River will be restored, long enough for a leisurely three to four day paddling journey. If you included the upper chain of lakes south of Orlando, it would be more than a hundred miles.

When we finished our site visits and said our goodbyes, I sought to visit the restored river at a live oak strand know as Bluff Hammock. Walking beneath the tree canopy on the Florida Trail, my feet crunching fallen palm fronds, I scared up deer and wild turkey. After about a mile, the trail opened up with a long boardwalk across a marsh. I was immediately struck by the majesty and power of the restored river before me. I climbed a small bridge as two immature yellow-crowned night herons playfully swooped past. An endangered wood stork soared across the main river channel. Birds have returned to the river en-masse since restoration efforts began.

The river was at flood stage, spreading out over a vast marshy expanse as it did historically for several months out of the year, and as I gazed across that moving, watery expanse—sensing its wild pulse—I gave silent thanks for all who had given of themselves to help restore this treasure. And for the first time, I gave thanks for the honor of writing the Kissimmee book. I felt it, deeply. The Kissimmee—its restoration and potential for visitors to have a wilderness experience—was much larger than any one person. It was a shared dream, a contract with nature that revealed the best of humanity. Who could ask for a better reward than to witness it being fulfilled?

In August of 2010, *New Dawn for the Kissimmee River: Orlando to Okeechobee by Kayak* was awarded a first place Excellence in Craft Award for an outdoor book by the Florida Outdoor Writers Association.

If You Go
The best way to keep track of efforts to develop a blue ribbon paddling trail through the Kissimmee chain of lakes and Kissimmee River is through the recreation section of the South Florida Management District website: http://www.sfwmd.gov/portal/page/portal/xweb%20protec ting%20and%20restoring/recreation. Currently, the most convenient spot to access the restored Kissimmee River by boat is to utilize the new 18-acre Istokpoga Canal Boat Ramp Area, open 24 hours a day, seven days a week. To reach it from the city of Okeechobee, travel north on U.S. Hwy 98 for approximately 25 miles to the Istokpoga Canal Bridge. At the Istokpoga Canal Boat Ramp Area sign, turn right into the facility. From Sebring at U.S. Hwy 27, travel south on U.S. Hwy 98 for approximately 17 miles to the Istokpoga Canal Bridge. At the Istokpoga Canal Boat Ramp Area sign, turn left into the facility.

A deer roams the Kissimmee prairie.

23

The Manatee Haven of Blue Spring State Park

"What a surprizing fountain must it be, to furnish such a stream, and what a great space of ground must be taken up in the pine-lands, ponds, savannahs, and swamps, to support and maintain so constant a fountain, continually boiling right up from under the deep rocks, which undoubtedly continue under the most part of the country at uncertain depths?"
--John Bartram, 1766, upon visiting Blue Spring

Blue Spring State Park near Orange City draws increasing numbers of manatees and people each year, but the first time I visited, I pulled into an empty parking lot just after dawn. I emerged from my car in the crisp air, anxious to stretch my legs, when a silver sedan pulled up beside me. A gray-haired woman behind the wheel whom I shall call Mary introduced herself and exclaimed how our two cars looked similar. I agreed, but I was more anxious to hike than to talk. Mary persisted as she emerged from her car.

What I learned as I fidgeted with my daypack and shoes was that for the past several years, Mary—a retiree—walked along the Blue Spring run almost every morning. By name, she came to know many of the manatees that frequent the springs in winter. They are distinguishable by the numerous boat propeller scars on their backs, and she produced photos of them that she showed off, as if they were grandchildren. I felt obliged to look at them. After all, how many people keep a photograph collection of individual manatees?

We talked about manatees for awhile, but she shifted the discussion and placed a different set of photographs in my hands. They were images of light hitting tree trunks a certain way, forming bright angel shapes. "You have to look quick," Mary said. "They don't stay long." She smiled a sweet smile, her blue eyes shining. Mary didn't seem elderly anymore. Perhaps she was one of the park's many citizen angels who watch over this vast expanse of water and trees.

After thanking her for sharing with me, I put on my daypack and turned to leave. "Look at the trees," Mary called after me. "You'll see angels."

I've been looking ever since.

But what I mostly search for—and find—at the 2,643-acre park is wildlife. First, there is the path and boardwalk along the one third-mile spring run leading to the largest spring on the St. Johns River. The 110-foot deep natural well pumps out more than 100 million gallons a day. If the weather has turned chilly and water temperatures in the river have dropped, the manatees congregate in the spring run and its 72-degree water. Sometimes, they are so numerous, it seems one can walk the length of the stream on their backs.

In 1970, two years before the park was established, researchers tracked 14 manatees in the spring run. Several boat houses stood along the spring run, boat use was common year-round, the banks were eroded, and manatees did not enjoy the same degree of protection they do today. By 2005, after years of park improvements and manatee protection efforts, wintering manatee numbers exceeded 200. And during the winter of 2010/2011, a record 344 different manatees—including 27 calves—visited the spring at least once.

The large pods of wintering manatees denude the spring run of water weeds. On one occasion, in 2008, they had encircled a fallen palm tree like cows around a hay bale and were trying to eat the tough fronds. Manatees were rising half way out of the water to grab a fresh branch. Squeaking noises of the coarse palm leaves going through the manatees' mouths filled the air.

Besides sea cows, fish abound in the spring run. There are mullet, tarpon, gar, bass, sunfish, as well as non-native tilapia and armored catfish. The abundant fish attracts a variety of wading birds, ospreys, eagles, and kingfishers. The park harbors at least 15 threatened or endangered plants and animals, including black bear, Florida scrub-jay and gopher tortoise. It is one of only two known locations for the rare Okeechobee gourd.

To see the park's wonders, one can hike along the spring run and the 4.5-mile Pine Island trail. Or, one can launch a canoe or kayak or rent one at the park. The adjacent Hontoon Island State Park offers further exploration by watercraft.

Wildlife viewing can also be enjoyed on a narrated nature and ecological guided tour provided by the St. Johns River Cruises. Captain Ron Woxberg and his staff dock two large passenger boats at the park. The newest one fits 60 people and has a lift for wheelchairs and a reserved area for wheelchair bound people and their companions. It is even AED (automated external defibrillator) equipped and certified should someone suffer a heart attack.

School groups take the boat tours as part of the Dip and Learn Science Fun Lab. They measure water temperature, salt content and turbidity. The older students utilize dip nets and view small animals under magnification. They study the food chain from larvae, shrimp, killifish, bass, catfish on up to human beings. Then, each student makes a presentation of their findings to fellow students, comparing results in the spring run with a river oxbow. "We can ramp it up or down depending on their education level," said Captain Woxberg, "but I'm always amazed at how quickly some of the students grasp the science. We've done it for elder hostels, too." A discussion of ways to prevent water pollution often follows the experiments.

During the 2009/2010 fiscal year, 21,000 people took the boat tours and park visitation topped a half million for the first time. The rising number of visitors is not surprising given the park's natural features and close proximity to large population centers. At times during the manatee season, the park reaches capacity, especially on weekends and special events. Visitors are advised to arrive early to ensure entrance, or seek to visit during the week.

And due to the abundant manatees in winter months, Blue Spring and the spring run are closed to scuba diving, snorkeling and swimming from mid-November through March 1st. The park's annual manatee festival is held each January. The park also features six rental cabins and a full-service campground.

But while the park's visitation and manatee numbers rise each year, there are worries that water volume in Blue Spring has been slowly dropping due to prolonged drought and increased water demand in the region. The Blue Spring Working Group, a coalition of springs experts and concerned citizens, has been formed to address issues concerning the spring and how to safeguard the basin.

Historically, Blue Spring has changed. In 1766, naturalist John Bartram observed that the spring was a "surprising fountain ... the colour of the sea, [that] smelled like bilge water, tasting sweetish and loathsome." Interestingly, the spring's sulfur odor and taste has since vanished.

In the 1800s, the area's virgin timber was harvested and the logs were hauled by steamship to Jacksonville, 150 miles away. In 1872, the Thursby family built a large wood frame house on a 3,000-year-old Timucuan shell mound overlooking the spring run and river and planted citrus. Louis Thursby set up a steamboat landing to ship goods and tourists to Jacksonville and beyond. The house still stands and is open to visitors as a walk-through museum, although the citrus trees are long gone. The riverine forest has recovered and visitors can glimpse scenes reminiscent of when Timucuan Indians lived along the spring run, complete with abundant wildlife. And if there was ever such a thing as a manatee telegraph, it has successfully touted Blue Spring State Park as a safe sea cow haven when the weather turns cold.

If You Go

Blue Spring State Park can be reached by driving thirty miles northeast of Orlando to Orange City on Highway 92/17. Turn west onto French Avenue and follow signs. For more information, log onto http://www.floridastateparks.org/bluespring/default.cfm. To reserve space on a river cruise, call 386-917-0724. Kayak and canoe rentals are available at the park.

Kingfisher with fish at Blue Spring State Park.

24
Paddle Florida: Eco-tourism at its Best

"Don't think I've laughed so much in many years. Was
just what my soul needed."
--Marcia Myers on her first Paddle Florida experience

The Ochlockonee River was up. A fierce storm two
nights before had created a swift waterway where a
lazy river had flowed. Mid-March was unpredictable that
way, but the sure thing thirty paddlers could expect on a
six-day, 76-mile journey from the Jackson Bluff Dam at
Lake Talquin to the Gulf of Mexico was spring beauty in
all its glory, and a wild river that primarily flows through
undeveloped conservation lands.

It was the first ever "Dam to the Bay" Paddle
Florida kayaking excursion. Paddle Florida is a non-profit

organization that got its start in 2008 taking large numbers of paddlers down the Suwannee River, working closely with area outfitters, local governments and the Florida Park Service. Since then the group has focused on sponsoring a trip in each of Florida's five water management districts. This would be its northwest Florida journey.

We gathered at Ed and Bernice's Fish Camp along Highway 20, twenty miles west of Tallahassee. The long time family-owned business is a large circular clearing of land along the river dotted with pavilions and a handful of motor homes. The camp normally caters to anglers in motorboats, but now it was decorated with colorful kayaks and tents. According to the owners, the bustle of activity would attract attention and more business.

As each paddler arrived, they received a t-shirt, a packet of information from different sponsors, a water bottle, and other goodies. Participants pay a registration fee and an optional meal plan fee. For this trip, the caterer was the Doobie Brothers Barbeque and Catering out of Bristol. The father/son team would have to set up their portable kitchen at three remote Apalachicola National Forest campgrounds, one Tate's Hell State Forest campground, and the group camp at Ochlockonee River State Park.

For each event, Paddle Florida spends between $4,000 and $22,000 on food alone, depending on the group's size. Add to that the costs for a large rental truck to carry gear, port-a-potties, gasoline, entertainment, campground fees and what each participant pays for food, gas and lodging before and after each trip, and Paddle Florida provides a boost to local economies.

While participants erected their tents or gathered in small groups to chat or paddle to the dam to wet a fishing line, I pored over maps with Bill Richards and Jan Corcoran, co-founders of Paddle Florida, and our trip leader, Ronny Traylor. Traylor is a retired recreation director for the Apalachicola National Forest and probably knows the river better than anyone alive. "My goal is for everyone to have a good time and not get lost," he said. "I've tied some pink and white flags at the confusing turns and side channels we'll need to take to our campgrounds. We just want everyone to stay in sight of the paddler in front and back."

Paddle Florida co-founders Bill
Richards and Jan Corcoran.

The Ochlockonee gives the appearance of a wide, easy flowing river from the Highway 20 Bridge, but it quickly narrows and becomes fast and tortuous in sections, with numerous side streams and sloughs. In places there are bluffs and long sandbars, and in others, thick river swamps dominated by cypress and tupelo gum trees with little dry land. Near the Gulf, the river widens and paddlers are greeted with vast salt marsh prairies and mazes of tidal creeks. A team of us had scouted the river the summer before, and Richards obtained the necessary special use permits for group camping from the agencies managing the campgrounds where we would stay. This was likely the first group of this size to paddle the river since Creek and Seminole Indians in the 1800s. It took some careful logistical planning.

Part of Paddle Florida is educational. Each evening there are lectures and/or musical entertainment. On this evening, we heard from Robert Lide with the Northwest Florida Water Management District, speaking of their efforts to restore the hydrology of Tate's Hell Swamp, and we also received safety instructions from Florida Fish and Wildlife Conservation Commission (FWC) officer Lane Bentley. On other nights, there would be talks about Florida's designated paddling trails, restoration of the Kissimmee River, and FWC recreation opportunities. Musical entertainment—a Paddle Florida mainstay—would be provided by folk singer Raiford Starke, often described as "the human jukebox".

Of course, the real showcase of any Paddle Florida trip is the featured waterway. When we embarked on a cool Sunday morning, the river cloaked in a rising mist, a bald eagle was perched in a tall snag and two otters playfully romped along the shore. Great blue herons flew overhead. Over the next several days, we would spot various ducks, alligators, turtles, water snakes, wild turkeys, woodpeckers, wading birds and graceful swallow-tailed kites. Endangered Atlantic sturgeon are now swimming up the river to spawn, but we didn't see any of the primitive looking fish leaping out of the water.

Plants, too, put on a show along the river as spring unfolded with each day—bright green cypress needles and gum leaves, red maple seeds, striking red bud trees and the white and pink blossoms of wild azalea. And with each day, our small community of paddlers became more cohesive. People grew closer through the long hours of paddling together, sharing meals and group camps, and in a few instances, rescuing each other after accidently tipping over in the river. Jokes and funny stories flowed freely. Previous or current professions didn't matter—fireman, physician, Army helicopter pilot, economist, contractor, commercial pilot, pharmacist, teacher, librarian, manufacturing engineer, dental assistant, substance abuse counselor—everyone was on equal footing.

Building community in an outdoor setting was what motivated Richards and Corcoran to create Paddle Florida. The idea first gelled in 2006 when they took a long distance paddling trip down the Suwannee River with two other friends. "About halfway through we determined that people would love to do this if they didn't have to carry their gear and cook their food," said Richards, who has a background in sports management and tourist development. The template for the logistics was modeled after the annual Paddle Georgia and Bike Florida trips. "We had 160 people on our first event down the Suwannee and I knew we were onto something," he continued. "When you think about it, it doesn't get any better than this for nature-based tourism."

Corcoran added, "I do this because I love paddling, love people, and I get out of the house. I enjoy getting to know a variety of people from all over."

On the Ochlockonee trip, there were numerous participants from the state of Florida—Jacksonville, Miami, Dunnellon, Inverness, Ponce Inlet, Naples, Sebastian, Eustis and Tampa—but there were also people from Georgia, Alabama, Louisiana, Virginia and Wisconsin. For its eleven trips and counting, Paddle Florida has had more than 350 different people from 26 states, and many repeat customers.

Paddle Florida camp scene.

Sharing a river he has known all his life is what motivated third generation Florida native Ronny Traylor of Bristol to volunteer as the trip leader. "This is an opportunity for people to explore a river they would normally not do on their own," he said at our last night's camp at Ochlockonee River State Park. "I love to see their faces as they discover new things and new places and hear their stories in the evening of what they've seen and experienced that day. I've enjoyed watching the community grow and see the interactions and the bonds that are developing. There is awesome camaraderie here, and we support each other."

Traylor paused for a moment as he scanned the golden marsh grass of the lower Ochlockonee floodplain. "I enjoy what I've had here all my life, but I enjoy it more when I can share it," he concluded.

Bill Detzner, a special education school teacher on spring break from Miami, appreciated Traylor and Paddle Florida for the opportunity to experience a river "I never even heard of before." He added, "This is a great place to see wildlife and to unwind and relax. It's a very calming experience to paddle along like this. I met a whole lot of new people and now have the resources to do this with my wife and friends on my own when I retire in five years."

On the trip's last day, we paddled towards the gaping mouth of the Ochlockonee Bay, the water a dead calm. The sun rose slowly through clear skies, a nearby osprey stirred in its bucket nest of sticks in a dead cypress snag, and unseen birds sang from the vast marshy expanse on either side of us. I paddled alongside a man I had met six days before. He confided to me that he had lost his older brother to a stroke just the day before and would be going to his funeral directly from the landing at Bald Point

State Park. After offering my condolences, I added, "Let's dedicate this beautiful morning to your brother." He wholeheartedly agreed.

After paddling quietly for awhile, the man relayed how they had fished this very river when he was a young boy and that his brother was a bit upset with him for catching the bigger fish. "He was fourteen years older," my companion said with a chuckle. "I think it hurt his pride."

"You need to share that story at the funeral," I suggested. He smiled and nodded.

After paddling beneath the mile long Highway 98 Bridge, we could see the spit of Bald Point ahead and the vast Gulf of Mexico beyond. This Paddle Florida journey was about to end, but I felt confident that many more would follow, and that the Ochlockonee River would again showcase its wild beauty to a growing community of paddlers.

If You Go

Ed and Bernice's Fish Camp can be accessed by driving about thirty miles west of Tallahassee on Highway 20. The camp is along a paved road a quarter mile southwest of the bridge. Signs clearly mark the way. There are no outfitters along the river, but canoes and kayaks can be rented in Tallahassee at Blue Water Sports (850-656-3483) and at The Wilderness Way ten miles south of Tallahassee (850-877-7200).

To learn more about Paddle Florida, log onto www.paddleflorida.org. To download a guide and map of the Lower Ochlockonee River Paddling Trail, log onto http://www.dep.state.fl.us/gwt/guide/designated_paddle/l Ochlock_guide.pdf. For more information about

Ochlockonee River State Park, easily reached by vehicle along Highway 319 just south of Sopchoppy, log onto http://www.floridastateparks.org/ochlockoneeriver/default .cfm.

Evening musical entertainment, such as Raiford Starke (above), is a mainstay of Paddle Florida trips.

25
More Than a Stream

"Springs nourish clues to our natural past, and they encourage us to recognize that what we have left is too precious to squander on hucksters who never sipped from a spring while keeping an eye on a crawfish at the bottom, or on a snake hanging off a tree limb overhead."
--Al Burt

As I descended a sandy hill of open piney woods, two deer crashed into the thick hardwood forest before me, almost seeming to escort me to Econfina Creek.

I heard the swift Florida Panhandle stream before I saw it. Numerous rapids, log strainers and hairpin turns mark this upper section, making it louder than most small Florida rivers and streams. For a canoeist or kayaker, the unique Econfina, especially the upper portion, is a roller coaster ride, suitable only for experienced paddlers. The creek races through clay, sandhill and limestone canyons it has carved over time, but can't seem to escape. But I came to hike part of the cross-state Florida National Scenic Trail that hugs the tall banks. On shore there was a calmer feeling, one of enchantment.

Walking along the copper-colored stream, I was awed by giant beech and magnolia trees. There were also spruce pine, red oak and white oak, hickory, and the twisted reddish trunks of sparkleberry.

Frequently pausing, I was fascinated by numerous swirls and eddies created by the current. The river's sweet song alternately faded or grew louder depending on the shape and width of a particular section. The banks became higher and steeper, often festooned with bright green moss and cascades of ferns. Tiny side streams also made music as they dropped into the main river channel. Some formed exquisite narrow waterfalls.

I passed more giant beech trees; carved initials were refreshingly absent. It was as wild and remote a hiking trail as one could find in Florida, and I was heartened by the fact that most of the surrounding land will remain undeveloped as part of the Northwest Florida Water Management District's 41,000-acre Econfina Creek Water Management Area (WMA).

Driving the project's strong preservation and conservation measures is the fact that the Econfina provides the lion's share of water to Deer Point Lake Reservoir, the primary drinking-water source for the Gulf Coast town of Panama City and surrounding environs. It is also a vital freshwater source for St. Andrew Bay, a vital nursery for marine life.

But it wasn't enough to simply protect the Econfina Creek corridor. Hydrologic testing found that almost 29,000 acres of sand hills west of the creek make up a major aquifer recharge area for several high magnitude springs that feed this vibrant watercourse.

Fortunately, the Water Management District was able to purchase most of this land from Rosewood Timber Company (Hunt Petroleum/Prosper Energy) of Houston for a little under $802 an acre in the 1990s.

George Fisher, retired senior planner for the water management district, was instrumental in the purchase. "It was a good price," he said, "but our future cost of restoring the uplands will be pretty heavy because they had been through a couple of timber cycles of sand pines; native vegetation was pretty much destroyed. Trying to reestablish it will really be a job."

Enter the nonprofit conservation group American Forests and their Global ReLeaf program. The water management district received 160,000 longleaf pine seedlings in 1996 and 195,000 longleaf seedlings in 1998 in an effort to restore the uplands. More longleafs were planted in subsequent years. This species of tree was once dominant in these and other uplands throughout the southeast, covering nearly 90 million acres. However, by most estimates a scant three percent of this habitat type remains due to logging, development, farming, fire suppression, and conversion to faster growing pines for paper production. The longleaf's dense yellow wood was prized for its ability to resist termites in the era before pressure-treated lumber. Only about 10,000 acres—featuring impressive pines 300 to 400 years old—are considered old-growth.

While most of today's longleaf forests are found on public lands, having grown back from forests cut in the early 20th century, private landowners are taking a new look at the longleaf pine's drought resistant qualities. A quiet longleaf revival is beginning to take root. Both public and private land managers throughout the southeast are planting so many longleaf seedlings that nurseries are having trouble keeping up with demand.

At the Econfina Creek WMA, seedling longleaf pines have now climbed out of the low-lying grass stage and are beginning to look like a young forest. Thousands of clumps of native wiregrass, a tall bunch grass that resembles baling wire, have also been planted. Wiregrass helps to spread fire more efficiently, an important component of the longleaf ecosystem since prescribed fires must now mimic natural fires that once swept through the uplands every one to three years. These slow creeping fires help to keep invasive hardwoods in check and also promote a lush understory that is necessary for several protected animal species. One of them, the gopher tortoise, is considered a keystone species since its deep burrows can provide homes for numerous species of frogs, mice, snakes and insects.

When fire approaches, gopher tortoises and similar animals race down their protective burrows. Other animals outrun the flames, climb high into the canopy, or simply fly away. Very few animals are caught in these slow-moving fires. The smell of smoke triggers a long ingrained sense of alarm.

Soon after a fire, herbivores such as deer, rabbits and gopher tortoises all gorge themselves on succulent new plant growth, and so their predators benefit as well. The plants attract insects and produce seeds and blossoms, and these, in turn, draw an array of bird life. One feeds the other.

Besides benefiting wildlife, William O. "Bill" Cleckley, Director of the Division of Land Management and Acquisition for the water management district, stated that in addition to benefitting wildlife, "The reintroduction of growing season prescribed fires to the restored landscape will induce flowering and seed production of remnant native groundcover plant species, which will significantly increase the biodiversity of the longleaf pine and wiregrass habitat." According to Cleckley, groundcover plant species richness could reach over 150 species per square hectare (about 2.5 acres), and at least 18 rare or endangered plant species now inhabit the upland sandhills of Econfina.

Longleaf forests such as this are being restored and protected on the Econfina Creek WMA.

Longleaf pines are the most fire-tolerant tree in the South, so frequent fires give them a competitive advantage over other trees. Their needles contain volatile resins that will burn even when damp. Longleafs can thrive in dry sandy environments since they sink a long taproot into the ground. Flames usually burn only the outer scales of their paper-like bark while the more fragile and vital inner layers are left intact. Even foot-tall longleaf pines, still in the "grass stage" because they resemble large clumps of grass, can usually withstand a fire. Burning green needles create a type of moisture shield for the plant's terminal bud. Generally only a very hot fire, one fueled by drought and a heavy build-up of fallen leaves and pine needles, will kill a young longleaf pine.

To gain a better understanding of what the recovering uplands of Econfina will one day look like, I took a stroll on the Florida Trail just west of the river. I first walked through a thick sand pine forest that had been planted by the previous owner. Then, through the trees, I could see what appeared to be golden prairie grass. Moving closer, I realized "the prairie" was a rolling hillside of feathery wiregrass in seed, the result of prescribed burning during the previous summer.

Wiregrass in seed can be three times taller than wiregrass that is not in seed. Scattered throughout the area were tall longleaf pines about a half century in age, one of the few remnant maturing longleaf tracts that the district was able to purchase. I was viewing the future of thousands of acres of young longleaf forest on the Econfina Creek Water Management Area. The recovering tracts will one day resemble "a prairie with trees," a description given by early pioneers who drove wagons through the vast, park-like expanses of longleaf forests.

Another unique environment found at Econfina is steephead ravines. Steepheads are like three-sided box canyons up to 100 feet deep that have small seepage springs and clear streams at the bottom. Steepheads erode from the bottom up as groundwater seeps through porous sand and leaks from an exposed slope. The sand above collapses and is carried away by the stream, so steepheads are continually cutting into the sandhill uplands. Since these shady wet environments are generally 10 to 15 degrees cooler than the dry uplands, steepheads harbor a unique array of plants and animals, including rare salamanders that often reside beneath mossy rocks and logs.

Besides obvious water supply/recharge, ecological, and recreational values, the Econfina Creek lands are valuable from a historical perspective. Early Native Americans lived there for millennia, from mastodon-hunting Paleo Indians to Muscogee Creek bands that moved in from Alabama and Georgia in the 18th and 19th centuries. Some native descendents remained in the area and have formed the Muscogee Nation of Florida, headquartered in a vintage one-room schoolhouse in the tiny town of Bruce about 20 miles west of Econfina Creek. The group, which has 1100 members, has been earnestly seeking federal recognition since 1978.

Early white settlers established a wagon trail through the hilly land along the creek country that one early observer called "the mountains of Florida." Perhaps the best known early pioneer was William Gainer. He settled along a group of large emerald springs that feed the river near present day Highway 20; the springs bear his name.

Gainer had been a scout and engineer for Andrew Jackson during his invasion of West Florida in 1818, and liked what he saw during the incursion. "This is a beautiful and productive place with great potential," he wrote to relatives in North Carolina soon after settling. "Tell our relatives and any close friends about it, but no one else." Gainer established a thriving plantation along the river, raising cotton, cattle and other farm products.

Eventually, large moonshine stills were pumping out white lightning along Econfina Creek and Deer Point Lake, a trade that was passed down through generations. As late as 1959, the average moonshine operation was believed to be producing 60 barrels a week.

While canoeing the calmer middle portion of the river one summer, I ran into Martha Barnes, a graying matriarch who had pioneer ancestors buried in a nearby cemetery. She was visiting one of the river's eleven clear azure springs. "I've been coming here since I was a kid," she said. "We used to play Tarzan and swing off the vines. There was no Highway 20 then; we used to come up on dirt roads. I bring my grandkids here now. I love the fact that it will remain wild and undeveloped."

It is not enough just to protect a paddling steam's immediate shorelines. A watershed approach must be utilized, and the recovering forests of the Econfina Creek Water Management Area is a testament to how it can be done.

If You Go

Learn more about the Econfina Creek Water Management Area and restoration efforts by logging onto http://www.nwfwmd.state.fl.us/recreation/econfinacreek.html. For more paddling information, log onto

. The easiest way to reach Econfina Creek and the many adjoining springs is on Highway 20 about 9 miles east of Highway 77 or about 7 miles west of Highway 231. A launch and parking area is on the northeast side of the bridge and the Pitt Springs Recreation Area can be accessed on the northwest side of the bridge. The Econfina Creek Canoe Livery (850-722-9032) can be reached by driving a short distance west of the bridge and traveling north about three miles on Strickland and Porter Pond roads, following the signs.

A youth jumps into one of Econfina Creek's many springs.

26
Wekiva Wilderness

"It was part fraternity house, part Jimmy Buffett-ville and, with kayakers and swimmers splashing in the river a few feet away, part Wekiva. ... One faction wants the languid river protected for hikers and paddlers who hold a deep appreciation for pristine serenity. Others want to experience the Wekiva as an awesome setting for volleyball, live music and 12 ounces of draft in a cup that readily biodegrades in sunlight."
--Kevin Spear, *Orlando Sentinel*, 9/4/2010, describing Wekiva Island

What does the Wekiva River ask of us? I wondered, as we tickled its surface with kayak and canoe paddles. Was our purpose to simply to enjoy its splendor, or was it something more long term?

During the first week in April, I joined four other friends on a three-day paddling trip. We embarked at the waterway's beginning at Rock Springs, just above Orlando. Immediately, we felt enfolded by arms of mature live oak trees festooned with resurrection fern. Arching palms, sweetgums and red maples rounded out the floodplain forest, all sprouting bright green spring growth. The tannin-tinted river was lined with dollar weed, water lily and pickerel weed, and beneath us, eel grass swirled in the gentle current. Fortunately, this upper section appeared to be without the invasive hydrilla water weed that has choked many Florida rivers and lakes. I hoped this stretch would be spared.

Water moccasin along Rock Springs Run.

Less than hour into the trip, a small ribbon snake swam before my kayak and I had to slow my craft to keep from running it over. Then, around a bend, we slipped past a water moccasin, partially coiled on a submerged branch. It eyed us closely, tongue flicking out to catch our scent, showing neither aggression nor fear. The same was true of most of the alligators and turtles sunning on logs. Many eyed us warily, but remained on their sun perches.

We stopped for the evening at Otter Camp, one of two primitive campsites established by the Wekiwa Springs State Park. The name for the springs and river, which simply means "a spring" in the Muscogee language, is spelled either "Wekiva" or "Wekiwa." Two more primitive campsites have been established by the Rock Springs Run State Reserve on the north side of the river. No-see-ums were abundant at Otter Camp and so were raccoons. The furry critters watched us from nearby palmettos, perhaps hoping we would be careless with our overnight storage of food.

Speaking of food, comparing my backpacking-ingrained minimalist tendencies with those of my paddling companions was easy, especially when I helped them load and unload their gear. For Mike and Julia, I had never seen so much food and gear loaded into 12-foot and 14-foot kayaks. There were three medium-sized coolers, a two-burner stove, a full cookware set and a large coffee pot. I carried some of it since I had extra space in my 17-foot kayak. Danny and Amanda, recently engaged, took a 16-foot canoe and they filled it with coolers and perhaps the largest plastic bin ever manufactured.

Setting up at Otter Camp, I pulled out my small propane stove and a pouch of freeze-dried chicken stew, while my companions set up a full kitchen. Soon, the aroma of sizzling vegetables and sautéed chicken and beef filled the still air. Fajitas were on the menu. "You want some?" Julia asked. "We have more than enough. I should have told you not to bring any food. Planning the menu is one of my favorite parts." I quickly put away my freeze-dried pouch and joined in. The difference between kayak camping and backpacking was starkly apparent, and I was the beneficiary of the lesson. There is no written or unwritten code that says you can't eat well while camping, so I partook guilt-free.

A lone Chuck-wills-widow and calling barred owls serenaded us to sleep that night, their voices echoing across the river corridor as they have for eons.

In the dream, I stood beside the wild river along its ancient shore, and I realized it could have been any time in the past few thousand years. The night birds were still calling. Otherwise, all was calm.

I sensed someone beside me, but couldn't see who it was. An unfamiliar woman's voice said, "The birds are answering your question."

"My question?"

"Yes, what you asked of the river."

"Oh, yes."

"They are saying that what they want of you is sustainability. They want you, humans, to be sustainable within ten years."

I nodded. It wasn't too much to ask—a reasonable request—and yet it was everything. For us to be sustainable as a species, it meant that places like the Wekiva River system could survive into the future because the planet as we know it would survive. Our insatiable desire for more of everything, especially of non-renewable resources, would be stemmed. And with lifestyle adjustments and a changeover to renewable energy resources, we could then live more compatibly with all of our relations. A tall order, but a necessary one.

To fail meant destruction. To succeed, harmony and beauty.

For our alarm clock the next morning, a hammering pileated woodpecker announced the dawn. Arising from my tent, I was greeted with a mist-cloaked waterway. A sweet smell permeated the air. Mystery was intermingled with wild beauty.

Once we were on the water again, blue damselflies landed on sunlit grape vine tendrils. Swallowtail butterflies flitted about blooming duck potato, blue flag iris and the white blossoms of titi. All was quiet and wondrous, until we neared the spring run coming out of Wekiva Springs and the main entrance to the state park. We soon encountered a steady stream of canoes and a few kayaks. We turned into the spring run and paddled slightly less than a mile to the headsprings in a quest to swim in clear spring water. It was here that we spotted hydrilla in abundance, rising up from the sandy bottom and nearly touching the surface. Excess nitrates in the springs and in most other Florida springs feed and boost their phenomenal growth rate. Regardless, people flock to the springs to cool off and marvel at their beauty, however tarnished.

Wekiva Springs on a warm Saturday afternoon was simply an extension of the historic spas and health resorts that once thrived along its high banks, except that more people now flock to the springs than ever before given the tremendous population explosion in the region during the past three decades. More than 1.3 million people currently live within 20 miles of the Wekiva River, and park visitation will surely continue to rise. In 2009, during the peak of the Great Recession, Florida's state park budget was slashed, and yet visitation rose to a record high—21.5

million visitors. You can spend a whole day at a state park for a few bucks versus the wallet-busting theme parks that have put Orlando on the tourism map. But the trend towards simpler leisure experiences can mean increased pressure on our natural environment.

Wekiva Springs can be busy with canoeists on weekends

If Wekiva Springs was crowded, nothing could quite prepare me for Wekiva Island (formerly Wekiva Marina), the location a commercial outfitter, bar and party spot perched on the water's edge just below the Wekiva spring run. Hundreds of people were enjoying the sun and spirits, and an Easter egg hunt was in full swing. While the family-owned establishment does boast rainwater-fed bathrooms and solar panels, canoes were streaming out of the place, and some canoes were filled with six people counting children. "Don't make me pull this canoe over!" screamed a mother to one of her restless brood.

Many of the paddlers were inexperienced, as evidenced by their zigzagging and bumping into trees, logs and each other. This section of the Wekiva is one of the most heavily canoed in Florida.

As the canoeists zigzagged up or down the river, they searched the shorelines for the rare alligator or turtle or wading bird that had given up trying to hide because they can't live life forever hidden, either underwater or deep in the swamp. At some point, many river animals have to come out to sun and feed, find a mate and raise young, despite the hordes of people who invade their domain, especially on weekends and holidays.

What quality of experience do these people have on the river? They get a glimpse, perhaps, as they paddle a mile or two upriver or downriver and turn around. They certainly have less of an impact than if they were in motorboats. And it's great that the young people have been torn away from their computers, television and electronic games for a spell, part of the "No Child Left Inside" movement. Still, such crowded scenes remind me of the people who hike the paved nature trails in national parks—a half mile loop and you've seen the overlook or waterfall or huge tree or whatever attraction the park is known for. Time to move on. By the sheer volume of people at these embarking points, it's as if we've established recreational sacrifice areas, at least during peak times.

On the springfed Weeki Wachee River along Florida's Gulf Coast just above the populous Tampa Bay area, the crush of people is even worse than on the middle Wekiva. There are just as many paddlers, but it's on a narrower and shallower stream. Throw in a hundred or so motorboats and throngs of swimmers, many of whom are leaping from trees, and you've got a mess. There's not much problem with hydrilla. That's because the boats and swimmers have scoured the bottom, preventing any growth in the channel. Wading birds, normally abundant during the week, have completely vanished. To where, I don't know. But manatees often make their way through the crush of boats and people until finding some sanctity at the boat-free zone at the head springs where only women in mermaid costumes perform to a human audience behind glass. It is difficult to feel intimacy or a close connection. Government bodies rarely have the courage to regulate boat use, except for some hotly contested manatee speed zones, but if ever there was a need for regulation, it would be in the upper Weeki Wachee River.

With the Weeki Wachee, the fragile balancing act between the needs and desires of people and the needs of the environment has clearly tipped in favor of people, and in the long run, our experiences on the river will be degraded along with the environment.

Overall, perhaps these recreational sacrifice areas do some good. Because millions have had a brief exposure to fresh air and natural beauty, there is majority support for managing lands and waters in their natural state, for protecting valuable wildlife habitat, for purchasing at-risk properties that are in harm's way, and for restoring those areas that were nearly ruined by short-sighted projects. Providing broad recreational access is a trade-off, especially when vast areas are left as wilderness with limited access. It doesn't mean I enjoy lingering in those crowded places, however. After Wekiva Island, I found myself paddling faster to reach that point where I knew most of the day paddlers would turn around. Two miles downriver, after passing countless paddle craft, there was almost no one, and it was apparent that the wildlife knew the safety zone, too. Their sudden abundance was obvious--more alligators, turtles and wading birds.

We spotted a lone manatee, about seven feet in length. It surfaced near our boats and followed us a mile or so downriver. Mutual curiosity. The sea cow had likely wintered in Blue Spring and other springs in the area. Now, as the water warmed, it was traveling to points unknown, probably into the myriad of lakes, creeks and other waterways within the St. Johns watershed, or possibly even to the coast or ocean more than 160 miles away.

When the manatee finally left us, a swallowtail kite cast an alluring spell. It swooped in front of us, inches above the water, stretched out its neck and opened its beak for a refreshing drink in mid flight. Then it circled and repeated the exercise several more times. If ever there was a bird that symbolized this stretch of river, it would be the swallow-tailed kite—quiet, gentle and graceful.

The vast majority of Wekiva paddlers see only a two-mile stretch of river near the canoe rentals. A smaller number seek to get away and experience a longer paddling trip, usually from Rock Springs to Wekiva Springs or from Wekiva Springs to Katie's Landing, a four to five hour journey. Just a handful each week embark on an overnight paddle, experiencing the many moods of the river for at least a 24-hour cycle. It's likely that a portion of the day paddlers yearn for something more, especially when they see fully loaded kayaks and canoes glide by with a look of wanderlust on the paddlers' faces.

Once on a quiet stretch of river again, I visualized the steamboats that once chugged up and down the river, carrying tourists and goods all the way to Rock Springs. Of course, the channel had to be dredged and snags removed during that time. And loggers had free rein in stripping the shoreline forests. I'd venture to say that the river and its recovering floodplain forest is wilder today than a century ago, with some snag openings only wide enough for a canoe or small john boat to pass through. Plus, there is no longer the random shooting of alligators, birds and other animals from steamboat decks. We have evolved as a species to some extent. The river also enjoys extra protection as one of only two national wild and scenic rivers in the state of Florida, joining the Loxahatchee. And unlike the Loxahatchee, the entire Wekiva river system is included in the designation.

Julia and Danny fish just before sunset.

Since Julia worked with the Seminole County Parks and Recreation Department, we received permission to camp at the county-owned Wilson's Landing Park. A primitive campsite has been planned for the future. Our campsite was a perfect spot on a small rise overlooking a wide stretch of river, and because of a steady breeze, the bugs weren't as plentiful as the night before. Danny wanted to try some fishing and he found a bass honey hole directly in front of the park's boardwalk. The fish were too small to keep, but Danny was thrilled and we shared in his excitement.

After dark, we made a small fire and took turns reading from Mike's book of Robert Service poems. Most were about the wild Yukon and they put us in a wilderness mood. How often do people get to sit around a fire and read poetry to each other?

The next morning, we passed several houses just below the Highway 46 Bridge, the only bridge crossing on the Wekiva. The river seemed to tame a bit, but it only took a couple of bends before wildness returned as we entered the Lower Wekiva River Preserve State Park and Seminole State Forest, prime bear habitat. So many bears inhabit the area that wildlife underpasses have been built along busy highways where bears are known to cross. Paddlers sometimes spot bears along the Wekiva River and I once spent a sleepless night camping in the Seminole State Forest because bears continually roamed through my campsite. By morning their scat was everywhere.

We didn't see any bears along the lower Wekiva on this trip, but we did spot numerous alligators and wading birds, including uncommon limpkins, and enjoyed watery panoramas and narrow canopied stretches. In all, Florida has protected more than 70,000 acres of the Wekiva River system. Few places in the country have rivers that emerge from a rapidly urbanizing area and almost immediately flow through vast tracts of wilderness. Decades of conservation land buying programs in the state have yielded impressive results, depriving developers of choice properties.

Wekiva protection efforts began in earnest in 1982 with the establishment of the Friends of the Wekiva River. Six years later, the environmental group spearheaded passage of the Wekiva River Protection Act, which helped to safeguard wetlands, wildlife and habitat, and rural character within a 180-square mile protection area. This opened the way for the federal wild and scenic river designation in 2000.

We followed the Wekiva to its terminus on the wide St. Johns River. I'd like to say that this famed north-flowing river—designated an American Heritage River by the United States Environmental Protection Agency because of its history and rich ecological values—was a highlight to savor, if only for a mile. But we were too busy dodging boats and their wakes to take it all in. A pretty Sunday afternoon was probably the worst time to hit the river.

A pontoon boat sped by followed by a sleek racing boat and a jet ski. These weren't as troublesome as the big cabin cruiser with the four-foot wake. I cinched my life vest tighter and wished I had brought my spray skirt. Given the choice, I would have gladly traded this for a couple of hundred canoeists who can't steer. I felt as vulnerable as a manatee, and it's no surprise that nearly a hundred sea cows a year are killed by speeding boats and nearly all manatees are permanently scarred by boat propellers. For millions of years, manatees have enjoyed life with few predators. Suddenly, they are faced with killing machines traveling at high speeds and they simply can't move out of the way fast enough. Coupled with annual cold weather deaths, biologists question whether current manatee populations can be sustained. With more than a million registered boaters in the state, and only a few thousand manatees, greater sensitivity and enforcement of slow speed zones are needed.

We weaved to and fro, having to turn our bows into the boat wakes. Fortunately, no one swamped and when we landed at the High Banks Landing, all was calm, mainly due to a no-wake zone around the ramp. I recalled the word from my Wekiva dream—sustainability. How can we sustain these enormous power boats in the age of peak oil? It left me with something to ponder. And it left me yearning for the peace of the Rock Springs Run and Wekiva River, where alligators and wading birds easily outnumbered motorboats and paddlers, even on a busy weekend.

If You Go

To learn more about the Rock Springs Run State Reserve, Wekiwa Springs State Park and the Lower Wekiva River Preserve State Park, log onto www.floridastateparks.org. Four primitive campsites for paddlers have been established by the parks. Additionally, primitive camping along the river is available at the privately-run Wekiva Falls Resort, 888 4 WEKIVA or 352-383-8055. For information about the Wekiva River/Rock Springs Run Paddling Trail, log onto http://www.dep.state.fl.us/gwt/guide/designated_paddle/Wekiva_guide.pdf.

Several outfitters are within twenty miles of the trail, including: Adventures in Florida (407-924-3375) http://adventuresinflorida.com/; Kings Landing (407-886-0859) http://www.kingslandingfl.com/; Wekiva Island, Inc. (407-862-1500) http://www.wekivaisland.com/; Wekiva Falls RV Park (407-830-9828); Wekiva River Haven Fish Camp (407-322-1909); Wekiwa Springs State Park Nature Adventures (407-880-4110) http://www.canoewekiva.com/ (last shuttle by 10 am, last rental by 3:30 pm; open 7 days a week); and Wekiva Adventures (407-321-7188) http://www.wekivaadventures.com/index.html.

A large Wekiva River alligator.

27
Florida's Mountain River

"The movement of a canoe is like a reed in the wind.
Silence is part of it, and the sounds of lapping water, bird
songs, and wind in the trees. It is part of the medium
through which it floats, the sky, the water and the shores.
A man is part of his canoe and therefore part of all it
knows. The instant he dips his paddle, he flows as it
flows, the canoe yielding to his slightest touch and
responsive to his every whim and thought."
--Sigurd F. Olson

Mist rose from the water as the Apalachicola River
coursed southward from the town of Chattahoochee
and the Jim Woodruff Dam in North Florida. The clear
morning—just cool enough for long-sleeve shirts—made
for perfect conditions to embark on a five-day journey. It

was 107 miles to Apalachicola Bay, so an early start was important for the twenty-plus mile days we would have to paddle to reach our goal.

The nature of this journey was different than most others. We were paddling to raise money for the Apalachicola Riverkeeper, a localized environmental advocacy group fighting for protection of the river and bay. Friends and relatives had donated money to the non-profit group on behalf of our group of six paddlers in a type of paddle-a-thon, and altogether we raised almost three thousand dollars. The venture was a brainstorm of area resident Earl Morrogh, who had paddled the river three times previously. We were also pleased to have then Riverkeeper executive director Andy Smith along with us. Andy had helped to coordinate Franklin County's response to the 2010 BP oil spill and this was his first real break in several months. Other paddling participants included Dona and Jack Carbone of St. George Island and Marianna paddling enthusiast Chris Matthews.

Remains of steamboat visible at low water.

Opposite the historic steamboat landing where we embarked lay the remains of one of more than a hundred early steamboats that plied these waters. Most often they made runs from Columbus to Apalachicola carrying cotton, tobacco, turpentine and other goods. And just downriver lay the mired rusting hulk of a barge, testament to more recent shipping days on the river when the Army Corps of Engineers sought to maintain a nine foot deep, 100-foot wide channel through dredging and snag removal. But maintenance dredging was halted by the state in 2005 because of cost, ecological damage, and the fact that a year-round channel deep enough for barge traffic was never achievable. Today, the river is primarily being used by anglers and a rising number of canoers and kayakers. The stone weirs and long rows of wood pilings known as "training fences" or "training dikes" to contain the channel, placed at key locations by the Corps, are largely guideposts of the past. The unimpeded Apalachicola River is slowly reverting back to its wild ways.

Even though the Apalachicola is Florida's top river in terms of water volume, and the twenty-first in magnitude of any in the lower 48 states, its primary threat centers around water quantity. A long standing water war has been occurring because farmers and the city of Atlanta continue to draw large amounts of water from the Chattahoochee and Flint Rivers—waterways that feed the Apalachicola—threatening the vitality of Apalachicola Bay and its multi-million dollar seafood industry.

Endangered river mussels and other organisms are also at risk from continually low water levels. The alarm sounded in 1990 when the Corps estimated that metro Atlanta water use was rising at the rate of 12.5 million gallons a day per year. The battle is ongoing with no real end in sight. For paddlers, the main advantages of low water are the sandbars. They were numerous, and they provided us with ample opportunities for rest stops and pleasant swims.

Just south of the Interstate 10 Bridge, we paddled alongside tall limestone bluffs along the eastern shore. Covered with large spruce pines and hardwoods, they gave the river an illusion of flowing through a more mountainous state than Florida. Appropriately, the Apalachicola is the only Florida river with mountain origins, emerging from the southern Appalachians via the Chattahoochee River. The Flint River, winding through Georgia foothills and flatlands, merges with the Chattahoochee at the Georgia border at Lake Seminole, forming the Apalachicola.

The Apalachicola has the tallest bluffs of any Florida river, and it also harbors several species of plants and animals normally found in the Southern Appalachians, including some species found nowhere else in the world. The river system is one of the most bio-diverse in the United States, harboring an impressive species list—60 trees, 1300 plants, 131 fish, 33 mussels, 308 birds and 57 mammals. It's no wonder that the Apalachicola has been called a national treasure.

We spotted a bald eagle perched on a tree, overlooking a broad floodplain, while a hawk's raspy cry echoed across the channel. They were the first of many raptors we would see throughout the journey and we would also spot numerous wading birds, alligators, turtles and deer. The river is largely undeveloped throughout its length, and thousands of acres of the watershed are in public ownership, providing valuable habitat for countless creatures.

Eagle drying wings along the Apalachicola River.

We passed several well known river landmarks on that first day. One was the Gregory House standing atop a bluff at Torreya State Park. I had never seen the mansion from the water. Originally, this Civil War era plantation house stood just downriver on the opposite shore at an old steamboat landing known as Ocheesee. The name comes from the Muscogee word for "hickory leaf" and it is believed that most of the former Creek inhabitants of the area were from the Hickory Ground settlement along the Coosa River in Alabama. During the Great Depression, CCC work crews dismantled the abandoned building and moved it to the park, where it was carefully restored and refurbished.

We lunched just below the park beside a gurgling stream that dropped into the river. It likely originated at a spring at the base of a three-sided earth canyon known as a steephead. Alligators sunned nearby alongside great egrets and great blue herons. Kingfishers zoomed across the river, giving their rattling calls, while bald eagles soared overhead. It was a day minted for paddling a river.

Our destination for the evening was another Apalachicola landmark—Alum Bluff. Towering more than 300 feet above the water, the white and orange clays and clinging trees made for an impressive sight, especially as the dipping sun cast the bluff in rich hues while we took in a late swim. The long sandbar where we camped was the perfect platform from which to view the bluff.

A herd of grunting wild pigs startled us as we sat around an evening fire. We didn't see them, but heard their crashing noises in the nearby woods. Later that night, coyotes howled and calling barred owls echoed across a moonlit waterway. Just before dawn, a barred owl in a tree just above our tents served as a fitting alarm clock. And so we readied ourselves for another adventuresome day. It was decided, at Earl's suggestion, to name the sandbar Camp Hoot and Squeal after its creatures.

Paddling along the Alum Bluff, cascading streams dropped into the river, another unusual sight in Florida. More bald eagles greeted us along with deer perched along the water's edge. We passed a handful of anglers who were having good luck catching catfish and crappie. Otherwise, the river was relatively quiet as far as humans were concerned. After 21 miles, we felt soreness in our arms and backs as we ended our day's trek at the bluff community of Estifinulga. The Muscogee Creek Indian name for the bluff means skeleton, or it may have meant

Spaniard clan, but a local story has it that a body once washed up on shore. "Hey, can you tell what kind of person it was" someone asked. "No, it's too stiff and ugly," was the response, and so the bluff is often called "Stiff 'n Ugly."

We named our sandbar camp "Stiff and Sore" after our condition. A full dinner graciously provided by Tallahassee restaurant TasteBudz and brought to us by Earl's wife Judye and their friend Joan lifted our spirits. The full moon rose as the sun set while we greeted the night with a warm fire and humorous stories.

We heard voices of a conversation from one of the houses on the bluff, neighbors talking while gazing upon the swirling Apalachicola River, their front yard. An eroding bluff can be a risky place to live. Estifinulga houses must occasionally be relocated landward while favorite trees eventually fall into the river.

Earl Morrogh has organized several paddling trips to benefit the Apalachicola Riverkeeper.

Embarking soon after the moon set and the sun rose, we paddled for several miles along undeveloped shorelines. Much of the land in this section is owned by the Neal Land and Timber Company, headquartered in Blountstown, while the state of Florida has purchased tens of thousands of acres of river floodplain in the upper and lower reaches of the river to protect water quality and wildlife habitat. More eagles soared overhead as we took rest breaks on long sandbars. We enjoyed following tracks of turkey, deer, raccoon, coyote, and at one spot, a large black bear. They come to the river to drink and perhaps to forage or swim, reaffirming that rivers such as this are lifebloods for wild animals.

Posted on trees along the river were numerous mile markers and reflective signs, a remnant of the barge traffic days. You can gauge your progress from the Jim Woodruff Dam at mile 107 to mile 0 at the town of Apalachicola. "That's a good news, bad news type of thing," Jack said at one point, resting on his paddle. "You can be amazed at how far we've come and feel somewhat alarmed at how far we have to go." The river was low and flowing at less than two miles per hour, so you couldn't just float and steer. Paddling was required.

We passed the halfway mark of the journey—53.5 miles—and ended the day sun-baked and tired at mile 42 at Gadsden Park in Wewahitchka. The town's name may mean "water view" or "the place where water was obtained" in the Muscogee Creek language, although some believe it means "water eyes" after the two oblong lakes along the town's edge. And the lyrical sounding "Apalachicola" either means "people on the other side" in the Hitchiti language or "allies" in the Choctaw tongue. Many Indian names were corrupted over time, leaving modern linguists to try to sort out the original spellings and meanings.

Riverkeeper board member and local author Michael Lister had dropped a truck and kayak trailer at the park so we could shuttle to the Dead Lakes Campground rather than navigate the four extra miles through the tricky Dead Lakes. The name emerged when the Apalachicola historically pushed a sandbar across the mouth of the Chipola, backing up water and killing thousands of cypress and gum trees. The dead trees still stand, ghostlike, giving the Dead Lakes a beautiful and somewhat eerie appearance.

In the dream that night, a mermaid swam up to my kayak and leaned on it, looking up at me with shining eyes. Sleek and otter-like, she was not green like in the movies or at Weeki Wachee Springs, but a gleaming brown—the color of the Apalachicola. "Swim with me," she said. She was part of the river, perhaps the spirit of the river, and she was beckoning.

Readying the kayaks the next morning, a man in a pickup stopped and asked about our journey. "Come join us," Chris offered, being polite.

"No way," the man replied. "I've seen alligators as long as those boats."

Below Wewahitchka, we passed a large number of houseboats tied along the shores. Many of these are hunting and fishing camps and some even had floating kennels for hunting dogs. We also passed one of the only high elevation points in this section--Sand Mountain. This towering hill—more than three stories tall and several acres wide—was one of many spots where the Army Corps of Engineers dumped sand from dredging operations. It now stands like a modern temple mound that is slowly being covered with plants and trees.

The river widened and a strong southeast wind grew throughout the day. That meant it was tough going for 24 miles to Hickory Landing Campground along Owl Creek. We wearily set up our tents in the pine-shaded campground, but Jeff Ilardi and his wife, Caroline, of the Riverkeeper board of directors perked up our spirits with a shrimp pasta dish from Café Con Leche in Apalachicola. While we ate, Jeff and Caroline kept entertained us with funny stories and cold beverages. Jeff, the board president, had a good time chiding Andy, the Riverkeeper's executive director, for his unshaven appearance. "Look at him," he kept saying, "he couldn't raise a nickel the way he looks." Andy had once worked as a river guide on mountain whitewater rivers such as the Chattooga and his appearance was quickly resembling that of a seasoned river guide again rather than an environmental lawyer and major fundraiser for the group. It doesn't take long on a paddling trip to "go natural" or "go native," and a few days of sun and no shaving can give guys a certain pirate look. Harrr. Interestingly, Andy would leave his job a few months later to return to river guiding, among other pursuits.

Then Jeff turned his attention onto me. "Are you Italian?"

"No."

"You've got to be Italian." He turned to the others. "Doesn't he look Italian?" Some nodded and others shrugged. He looked back at me with a penetrating gaze. "Are you sure you're not Italian?"

"I'm sure," I said, "but you can adopt me and feed me." I certainly enjoyed Italian food.

After our guests left, the challenge was to stay awake past dark. That's what hours of paddling in the fresh air does to a person.

On the last day—another 24 miler—the morning was dominated by light rain, distant thunder, and strong wind gusts. We struggled south to our destination as we passed the site of Fort Gadsden on the eastern shore. This is where escaped slaves, free blacks and Seminole Indians once held an abandoned British Fort until a battle in 1816 when an American warship lobbed a red hot cannonball into the fort. It struck the fort's magazine and the resulting thunderous explosion killed nearly all of the fort's 320 occupants. "The explosion was awful and the scene horrible beyond description," the American commander, Colonel Clinch, reported a short time later. It was perhaps the most significant single cannonball shot in early American history and it was a blow to the hopes of freedom for many escaped slaves.

As we hugged the shores of the broadening river, we noticed that cypress and tupelo gum trees had become prevalent. The region is famous for its tupelo honey, an industry highlighted by the 1997 movie *Ulee's Gold* starring Peter Fonda. Other trees included sweetgum, river birch, willow, water hickory and sabal palm. The sweet aroma of willow permeated the moist air.

Around Mile 16, we aimed towards a distant blue sky to the south, giving us renewed hope for good weather to finish the trip. It was as if the storms had skirted around us and we felt extremely fortunate. As we paddled the last miles, I thought of the many rivers I have paddled throughout my half century. Many stand out, but my favorite? It's usually the last one I paddled. It's an easy infatuation, given Florida's broad range of outstanding paddling trails, but to truly love a river requires repeated journeys. For Earl, this was his fourth thru trip on the river and he is committed to its protection. He vowed to organize more of these trips to spread awareness and to raise more money for the Apalachicola Riverkeeper. Dynamic rivers such as the Apalachicola inspire that type of commitment.

Once the weather cleared and the water turned to a glassy calm, the choice was to experience the intimacy of the shoreline or to paddle the main channel and feel the powerful expansiveness of the river. I alternated my choices, depending on which way the river was turning. The earlier cloud cover had caused the weather to stay cool well past noon, and Earl commented how it felt like we were experiencing an extended morning. Rivers can have many moods.

By mid-afternoon, shrimp boats came into view along with the five-mile Apalachicola Bay Bridge. Our trip would soon be over. I knew I would miss this broad waterway with its intriguing history, high bluffs and rich wildlife. I vowed to return and deepen the connection.

If You Go

The Apalachicola Riverkeeper is spearheading efforts to develop a paddling trail guide and maps for the Apalachicola River. Log onto their website to follow the progress, http://www.apalachicolariverkeeper.org/.

To reach the boat ramp at the Clyde Hopkins Park in Chattahoochee, simply turn south off of Highway 90 onto River Landing Road just east of the Apalachicola River Bridge. The road will wind down to the landing after a short distance. Numerous other landings are spaced along the river and side streams. The Apalachicola

Riverkeeper leads day kayak trips on the river, usually on the fourth Saturday of the month, and the Apalachicola Maritime Museum organizes kayak and canoe educational adventures on the lower Chattahoochee and Apalachicola rivers, http://www.ammfl.org/RiverTrips.htm.

Bear tracks lead to the Apalachicola River.

Early morning camp along the river while the moon sets.

28
Pelican Island Pilgrimage

"Year after year these birds return to Pelican Island. This regular return to the same island, which is no different and no more attractive than dozens of other islands along the same coast, is one of the curious things in bird life. It may be that they come here for sociability, just as humans congregate in cities. It may be that some instinct tells them this is a safe place to rear their families. At any rate, they are not easily frightened and will permit a cautious visitor to approach quite close to the nests."
--Nevin O. Winter, *Florida the Land of Enchantment*, 1918

Every paddler should make a pilgrimage to Pelican Island. The tiny mangrove-covered chunk of land in the midst of the Indian River Lagoon near Sebastian is where the greatest wildlife refuge system in the world began in 1903. President Theodore Roosevelt, an avid hunter and bird lover, heeded the cries of ornithologist Frank Chapman and other conservationists by protecting the last known brown pelican rookery on the East Coast. Plume hunters had devastated the rest. A line was drawn in the sand in an effort to stem the tide of wanton wildlife destruction, before it was too late for the brown pelican and many other species.

Today, Pelican Island has admittedly lost a bit of its former grandeur. From 5.5 acres and 5,000 pelican pairs in the early days, the island has eroded down to 2.2 acres and less than one hundred pelican pairs. Fortunately, brown pelicans have repopulated old haunts along with newer spoil islands in establishing several other rookeries. Part of their success is because Pelican Island was protected and used as a launch pad for expanding bird populations.

I had the opportunity one evening to kayak to Pelican Island. Only a few pelicans were visible around the island, and some were perched atop posted signs planted in the water along the perimeter, warning visitors to stay back. But despite battling fifteen-knot winds whistling across the wide Indian River, I relished the isolated feeling of the place. Surrounding lands have been protected and I saw no one else, not even a motorboat. A mullet nearly leaped into my boat, and I scared up an unidentifiable large marine creature, perhaps a manatee or huge fish.

While boaters and paddlers must stay a safe distance from the island's nesting pelicans, Frank Chapman set up a blind on the island in 1905 and wrote down his observations for *The Century Magazine*: "Birds of all ages and voices, from the grunting, naked, squirming new-born chick, or the screaming, downy youngster, to the silent, dignified, white-headed parent, were now within a radius of a few yards. At a glance, I could see most of the activities of pelican home life: nest building, laying, incubating, feeding and brooding young, bathing, preening, sleeping, fighting—all could be observed at arm's length. Surely here was a rare opportunity to add a footnote to our knowledge of animal life."

Paddling back to land as the sun dipped low and the east wind kicked up, the reality of what began on that tiny island hit me. From its humble beginning, 540 national wildlife refuges, representing almost 100 million acres, have been established. Refuges are now found in all 50 states as well as American Samoa, Puerto Rico, Virgin Islands, Johnson Atoll, Midway Atoll and several other Pacific islands.

In Florida, federal refuges include familiar names such as Pine Island, established 1908; Cedar Keys, 1929; St. Marks, 1931; J.N. Ding Darling, 1945; National Key Deer, 1954; Lake Woodruff, 1963; St. Vincent Island, 1968; Lower Suwannee, 1979; Crocodile Lake, 1979; Crystal River, 1983; Florida Panther, 1989; Archie Carr, 1991; Lake Wales Ridge, 1994; Ten Thousand Islands, 1996.

How many species of wildlife have benefited from those protected havens of land, and how many people have grown to appreciate them?

The Pelican Island refuge—the first of its kind—may not have happened at all if it weren't for the determination of German immigrant Paul Kroegel. In the late 1800s, before state or federal laws were enacted to protect non-game birds, Kroegel would sail out from his Sebastian house that was perched high atop an Ais Indian shell mound and stand guard on the island, gun in hand. He had had enough of watching birds slaughtered for their plume feathers, or simply shot for "fun" by passengers on passing steamboats.

In 1901, Kroegel became one of four Florida wardens hired by the Florida Audubon Society to protect birds. And after the island received its federal protection, he became its first manager. His initial salary: $1 a month. But a presidential executive order still wasn't enough to protect Pelican Island. Commercial fishermen, viewing the pelicans as a threat to their livelihood, were able to sneak onto the island in 1918 and club to death more than 400 defenseless pelican chicks. The threat abated after the Florida Audubon Society convinced the fishermen that pelicans primarily feed on non-commercial baitfish.

Mother Nature dealt the island a blow in 1923 when birds abandoned the island after a hurricane. Kroegel was soon retired from federal service and the island was without a manager until the mid 1960s, even though many of the birds had returned.

The island was again threatened in the 1960s when developers sought to build on adjacent islands and wetlands. Local citizens, including commercial fishermen, citrus growers and sportsmen, joined forces to form the Indian River Area Preservation League. They, along with Audubon of Florida, convinced the state to add 422 acres to the refuge. More land was acquired in the 1990s. The purchases allowed for a viewing tower to be built on adjacent land in 2003, marking the 100th anniversary of the refuge's establishment. The current refuge acreage stands at 5,413.

Steps to the viewing tower are emblazoned with the names of each refuge within the national wildlife refuge system and the year they were established, reminding visitors that Pelican Island is more than an island with a few birds. As long as a piece of it still protrudes from the water, it stands as a testament to the time when the human species tempered its hard-driving temptation to destroy that which is defenseless and beautiful. The island marks a milestone for our species, and it gives us hope for our own survival.

Here's how Frank Chapman concludes his 1905 article about the island: "Man alone appears to threaten their continued existence, and from him, fortunately, those of their kin who live on Pelican Island are now happily protected. While they cannot repay their defenders with the music of thrushes or a display of those traits which so endear the higher animals to us, they may at least claim success in filling their place in nature, while the charm of every water-scene is increased by the quaint dignity of their presence."

If You Go

Three different access points enable paddlers to launch kayaks or canoes to visit Pelican Island along Florida's east coast. A launch on Wabasso Causeway is about three miles to the south. Northwest of the island by about two miles is the Sebastian Park launch in Sebastian on the west side of the Indian River Lagoon. Just over four miles to the north on the east side of the lagoon is a launch at Sebastian State Park. Outfitters in the area offer kayak and canoe rentals and guided trips, the closest one being the Florida Outdoor Center in Sebastian, 772-202-0220.

Besides brown and white pelicans, other bird species that utilize the island for roosting, nesting or feeding include the double-crested cormorant, roseate spoonbill, wood stork, Forster's Tern, blue-wing teal, white ibis, American oystercatcher, anhinga, red-breasted merganser, ring-billed gull and various egrets and herons. The Pelican Island Wildlife Festival, commemorating the birthday of Pelican Island and the National Wildlife Refuge System, is held every March.

The refuge's boardwalk shows names of all 540 national wildlife refuges.

29
Clear Lake

"I do not know how anyone can live without some small
place of enchantment to turn to."
--Marjorie Kinnan Rawlings

It is hard to believe a place can hold such strong
memories when, if added together, my time at Clear
Lake would be only a handful of days over more than
three decades. Yet, on the banks of this small lake in north
Florida's Apalachicola National Forest, I can vividly
recall my first Boy Scout campout. I was eleven. Having
just moved from the Chicago area, everything was new to
me.

After dark, when we were busily putting bisquick dough on sticks and roasting them over a fire, two college-aged fishermen approached our camp. I'm not sure how the subject came up, but it turned out that these two were judo experts, or so they claimed. We arranged to have a contest—our twenty or so boy scouts, ages eleven to sixteen, versus the two of them. We scoffed. The odds were in our favor, and they weren't that big; we'd easily have them whipped. We ditched the bisquick and built up the fire to shed light on the imminent contest. The air felt charged, as if lightning were about to explode.

The two wiry young men crouched back to back while we circled, wolf-like, in search of an opening. Different boys suicidally rushed in, and were quickly flipped to the ground. Dust arose in swirls and stuck to sweaty bodies. "Rush 'em all at once!" exhorted my brother David, one of the older boys. But we would never rush at the same time. We were too hesitant, too chicken. As a result, we were flung around like wet sleeping bags until, red faced, we conceded to the heroic duo. The bruises and hurt pride from that night have long faded, but the memories—ones that have grown fonder with time—persist.

Clear Lake. The night my daughter was born in 1986, a group of friends held a vigil there. They camped out, sang, prayed. The next morning, they came to the hospital room, their clothes bearing the sweet smell of wood smoke, and sang "Happy Birthday" to Cheyenne. Whenever I visit Clear Lake, I can visualize that group of warm folks around a fire during a night when I held a wet crying newborn, tears streaming down my face. At Clear Lake, those tears of relief and joy return to me, and I give thanks again for Cheyenne's safe passage, and for the support.

The physical appearance of Clear Lake has changed little over time. Irregular in shape, the often still surface resembles a landscape painting. Tall encircling slash pines give it a North Woods appearance. Titi and St. Johns wort crowd the immediate shoreline while flat green saucers of lily pads grace the shallows. In late spring, water lilies poke out like serpent heads, cloaked in leathery green and purple husks. Once above the water's surface, the protective sheaths fall away, unveiling expansive white flowers with iridescent yellow eyes. They seem like windows to the lake's soul, deep and bright; breezes caress the soft petals while rippling the liquid mirror.

Biologists label Clear Lake a sand hill lake because it is nestled in dry piney sand hills where, millions of years ago, seashores created rows of sand dunes. Beneath layers of living and decaying water weeds, there is a sandy bottom. Although the water depth is no more than ten feet at the deepest spot, I've never seen Clear Lake dry up, even in the worst drought. There is no boom and bust cycle of fish and wildlife. Its waters are dependable.

A steady chorus of red-winged blackbirds are found at Clear Lake along with egrets, herons, songbirds, croaking frogs and, during warmer months, dragonflies and an assortment of other flying insects. I've never swum there, but I've canoed the lake and wet a fishing line a time or two. No fish ever sampled my bait or lure.

Clear Lake always looks perfect for fishing. Lily pads, marsh grass and bog buttons grow along the edges, logs seem to be located in strategic spots, and scores of minnows are active in the shallows. Occasionally, I've heard splashes of larger fish. After several attempts, and no fish, I stopped bringing my fishing rod. Perhaps Clear Lake is too pristine for fishing. Taking home a bass or bream from Clear Lake would be like accepting a valued gift from a close friend, relinquished only because of the value placed on your friendship. A gift that hurts a little, a gracious sacrifice.

I've been to Clear Lake in dreams. A friend is sometimes there with me and we walk along the shore discussing a subject that needs clarification.

I've camped at Clear Lake with my family, sat around a campfire, made the obligatory s'mores. I've also come alone, seeking solace. I would roam about, sit, be still, watch, listen, absorb. By the time I was ready to leave, I felt clearer and somehow cleaner of thoughts and vibes, more appreciative of family and friends. A healing tonic. Clear Lake has a softening effect.

I've fretted over Clear Lake. In the late 1970s, representing an environmental group, I attended a Forest Service workshop that sought to identify roadless areas that might qualify for federal wilderness designation. Among other areas, I nominated Clear Lake and its environs. Afterwards, a Forest Service employee took me aside. "I can understand Mud Swamp and places like that," he said, "but Clear Lake? It's got roads running through it, and it's all second-growth forest."

"But it's mostly uplands," I replied, "primarily longleaf pine. We don't have much of that in the wilderness system. Plus, there's the lake."

Seeing my determination, the forester grimaced. I was surprised the man didn't have sawdust coming out of his boots. Those were the days when the Forest Service in Florida was cutting large swaths of upland longleaf forest in the name of multiple-use management, before their more recent focus on ecosystem restoration. The slash and longleaf pines around Clear Lake were ripe for cutting, something I sought to prevent.

My motives for preservation weren't entirely altruistic. I focused on future generations, like most conservationists, but I also wanted to grow old with those trees and witness former logging roads revert to hiking and animal trails. Plus, there was the lake. I didn't want another developed recreation area where one has to drop money into a slot for the right to gaze upon the birthright of every American.

It is fortunate that Clear Lake lies in Leon County and not in the poorer Wakulla or Liberty counties. National forest timber revenues amount to a miniscule portion of Leon County's budget, and as a result, the Leon County Commission and many of its citizens supported inclusion of the 5,635-acre Clear Lake Area into the national wilderness preservation system. Consequently, the Forest Service and Congress only balked part way by designating it an official wilderness study area, a designation that persists.

Clear Lake is just far enough away from population centers to not be overrun, especially by the swimming and partying crowd. There isn't much of a beach, only enough cleared space to launch a small boat or canoe. I've seen other sand hill lakes closer to town turn into nudist colonies of a sort, where most people wear no clothes, and booze and drugs are commonplace. I pray it doesn't happen at Clear Lake. Occasionally, I've found strewn bait and beer containers near the landing. Other lakes fare much worse.

Hopefully, Clear Lake will one day be the liquid heart of a designated federal wilderness area. The surrounding forest will grow older and wilder, with man's influence minimized to igniting prescribed fires that mimic the frequent natural fires that once swept through the uplands before roads and fire suppression.

I like to think of Clear Lake's maturing trees as being a vital oxygen bank for the planet, like the Amazon rainforest on a small scale. Trees do more than simply look pretty.

Let Clear Lake remain a keeper of pure memories, a place for the dreamscape, where a soul can fly with the red-tails and float like a rippling breeze over water. Keep Clear Lake clear.

If You Go

Clear Lake is only about 10 miles southwest of Tallahassee. Take Lake Bradford/Springhill Road (County Road 373) past the airport for five miles and turn right onto Tom Roberts Road (Forest Road 305). This road will take several sharp turns for almost two miles until you reach a fork at Forest Road 307. Take a left and Clear Lake will be on your right after a quarter of a mile. An Apalachicola National Forest map is recommended.

30
What We Pass On

"There is sufficiency in the world for man's need but not for man's greed."
--Mohandas K. Gandhi

Sometimes, the water's pull is just too great. Even with questionable weather, and on Christmas Eve, I strapped a kayak onto my car and set out for a water body with my family's blessing.

I was soon paddling through a coastal cypress and gum swamp on a winding tidal creek off the lower Ochlockonee River. Despite fifteen mile-an-hour gusts, I sang "Glory Hallelujah" to mark the occasion. The sky was overcast, but the day seemed bright.

Because this stream was near the coast and more susceptible to hurricanes and sea level rise, and also due to the winter season, the shoreline bore a stark appearance. Many trees were dead, bleached and devoid of small branches. Woodpeckers had riddled several with cavernous holes. Other trees had simply shed their leaves or needles, to rest, so to speak, until warmer and longer days. There were exceptions, however. The eastern red cedar trees stood out. Their bright greenery along this waterway reminded me of a Muscogee Creek Indian story.

After Creator made the earth and its creatures, He rested and slept for a long while under a cedar tree. The cedar sheltered him and absorbed his breath, and so when cedar needles or wood is burned as incense, the sacred breath of Creator comes forth. Creator also rewarded cedar for sheltering Him by allowing the tree to be green year-round.

Two hooded mergansers flew just ahead, landing and swimming, then flying around the next bend. A flock of red-winged blackbirds landed on cypress branches and fetterbushes, noisy and gregarious. An osprey nest seemed to mark every turn in the dark twisting waterway, although I didn't spot any of the fish hawks. Perhaps the wind had them hunkering down.

The ospreys along the creek were likely the second or third generation of raptors since the late 1970s, the last time I had paddled the stream. The ospreys likely stayed because the brackish waters yield abundant quantities of salt and freshwater fish, or maybe they simply stayed because it has been home for countless generations of ospreys for millennia. No reason to leave a good home.

During that last outing, I had joined a local group from the Sierra Club, an organization with which I was active. All of us paddled canoes then; kayaks were an exotic novelty. I was a young adult of nineteen or twenty, and most of the people with me were gray-haired and far more knowledgeable than I about a great many things, especially about birds and the natural world.

Most of them are gone now—Jack Deasy, Eleanor Moore, Betty Watts, Tom Morrill, Jerry Carter, Inez Frink, Jim Hardison, Shirley Taylor, Ellen Winchester, Chandler and Helen Jones. They were my elders, and they were also my friends. By returning to the creek, I felt their presence again. The fact that it was as wild as I remembered—completely devoid of houses—was a testament that they and others of their generation did a good job of passing it on to the next one. And so while I paddled and recalled their legacy, my responsibilities came into clearer focus. I thought of others—especially young people—I hoped to take there and places like it in the future, to imbue in them a sense of stewardship. I yearned to become a responsible elder one day so the cycle could continue.

We have no guarantee as to how long we will live in this physical existence, but when it is my time to pass on, perhaps a place like the wild creek is where I want my ashes to be spread—certainly in water—to be carried out to sea and become part of the great cycle of life. That would symbolically and literally renew the feeling of oneness I have enjoyed, often while paddling.

We can rarely improve upon Creator's work, just simply admire and protect. Like the cedar, maybe the longer our exposure to natural beauty, the more we become part of Creator's breath and live on in His works.

If You Go
The tidal creeks along the lower Ochlockonee River can best be accessed from Ochlockonee River State

Park along Highway 319 five miles south of Sopchoppy.
A Top Spot waterproof map for the region or aerial
Google Earth photos can aid in navigation.

Bibliography

Balfour III, R.C., *In Search of the Aucilla*, Valdosta:
Colson Printing Co., 2002

Belleville, Bill, and Jim Robison, *Along the Wekiva River*,
Mount Pleasant, SC: Arcadia Publishing, 2009

Bishop, Nathaniel H., *Four Months in a Sneak-Box*,
Boston: Lee and Shepard, 1879

Burnett, Gene M., *Florida's Past, Volume 1*, Sarasota:
Pineapple Press, 1986

Carr, Archie, *A Naturalist in Florida*, New Haven and
London: Yale University Press, 1994

Carter, Elizabeth, and others, *A Canoeing and Kayaking
Guide to Florida*, Birmingham: Menasha Ridge
Press, 2005

Eidse, Faith, *Voices of the Apalachicola*, Gainesville:
University Press of Florida, 2006

Farrington, Brendan. "Florida Lighthouse Lost to the Sea
Now Stands Again." 7/28/2008. USA Today
website,
http://www.usatoday.com/travel/destinations/2008-
07-28-cape-st-george-lighthouse_N.htm.

Florida Office of Greenways and Trails, *Florida
Circumnavigational Saltwater Paddling Trail
Guide*, 2nd Edition, Tallahassee, 2010

Foster, Nigel, *Guide to Sea Kayaking in Southern Florida*,
Guilford, CT: Globe Pequot, 1999

Jumper, Betty Mae Tiger, and Patsy West, *A Seminole Legend: The Life of Betty Mae Tiger Jumper*, Gainesville: University Press of Florida, 2001

Leda, Loretta Lynn, *Paddling Everglades National Park: A Guide to the Best Paddling Adventures*, Guilford, CT: Falcon Guides, 2009

Leonard, Irving A., editor, "A Lost 'Psyche': Kirk Munroe's Log of a 1,600 Mile Canoe Cruise in Florida Waters, 1881-1882," *Tequesta*, XXVII (1968)

Matschat, Cecile Hulse, *Suwannee River: Strange Green Land*, New York: Farrar and Rinehart, 1938

McCarthy, Kevin, *Apalachicola Bay*, Sarasota: Pineapple Press, 2004

McKay, D.B., editor, *Pioneer Florida*, Tampa: Southern Publishing, 1959

Missall, John and Mary Lou Missall, *The Seminole Wars*, Gainesville: University Press of Florida, 2004

Oppel, Frank and Tony Meisel, editors, *Tales of Old Florida*, Secaucus, NJ: Castle, 1987

Rawlings, Marjorie Kinnan, *South Moon Under*, New York: Charles Scribners Sons, 1933

_____. *The Yearling*, New York: Charles Scribners Sons, 1938

Read, William A., *Florida Place Names of Indian Origin and Seminole Personal Names*, Tuscaloosa: University of Alabama Press, 2004

Smith, Shana, "Sierra, Florida Press Clubs Honor Peter Gallagher for Protecting Canoes in Newnan's Lake," Communigator Online Edition, Spring 2002, http://www.jou.ufl.edu/pubs/communigator/spring2002/Gallagher.htm.

Snyder, Bill, "They Call It Tate's Hell," *Florida Wildlife*,
    June 1950, pages 6-7, 17

Snyder, James D., *Life & Death on the Loxahatchee: The
    Story of Trapper Nelson*, New Revised Edition,
    Jupiter, FL: Pharos Books, 2004

Spear, Kevin, "Does Bar Hurt Wekiva River or Let More
    Appreciate It?" *Orlando Sentinel*, 9/4/2010,
    http://www.orlandosentinel.com/business/tourism/o
    s-wekiva-party-place-controversy-
    20100903,0,5566059.story.

Stamm, Doug, *The Springs of Florida*, 2nd Edition,
    Sarasota: Pineapple Press, 2008

Tebeau, Charlton W., *Florida's Last Frontier: The
    History of Collier County*, Coral Gables: University
    of Miami Press, 1977

_____. *Man in the Everglades*, second revised edition,
    Coral Gables: University of Miami Press, 1968

United States Fish and Wildlife Service, "Pelican Island
    National Wildlife Refuge," website accessed
    8/5/2010, http://www.fws.gov/pelicanisland/.

_____. "St. Vincent National Wildlife Refuge," website
    accessed 12/7/2010,
    http://www.fws.gov/refuges/profiles/index.cfm?id=
    41650.

Watts, Betty M., *The Watery Wilderness of Apalach,
    Florida*, Tallahassee: Apalach Books, 1975

Winter, Nevin O., *Florida: The Land of Enchantment*,
    Boston: The Page Company, 1918

3197288R00161

Made in the USA
San Bernardino, CA
15 July 2013